101 Businesses

You Can Start With Less Than

One Thousand Dollars:

For Students

Heather L. Shepherd

101 BUSINESSES YOU CAN START WITH LESS THAN ONE THOUSAND DOLLARS: FOR STUDENTS

Copyright © 2007 by Atlantic Publishing Group, Inc.
1405 SW 6th Ave. • Ocala, Florida 34471 • 800-814-1132 • 352-622-1875–Fax
Web site: www.atlantic-pub.com • E-mail: sales@atlantic-pub.com
SAN Number: 268-1250

ISBN-13: 978-0-910627-90-0   ISBN-10: 0-910627-90-8

Library of Congress Cataloging-in-Publication Data

Shepherd, Heather Lee.
  101 businesses you can start with less than one thousand dollars : for students / by: Heather Lee Shepherd.
     p. cm.
Includes bibliographical references and index.
ISBN-13: 978-0-910627-90-0 (alk. paper)
ISBN-10: 0-910627-90-8 (alk. paper)
1. New business enterprises. 2. Small business--Management. 3. Students--Employment. 4. Self-employed. I. Title. II. Title: One houndred one businesses you can start with less than one thousand dollars. III. Title: One hundred and one businesses you can start with less than one thousand dollars.

  HD62.5.S534 2007
  658.1'1--dc22
                        2007029736

Printed on Recycled Paper

EDITOR: Tracie Kendziora • tkendziora@atlantic-pub.com
INTERIOR LAYOUT DESIGN: Vickie Taylor • vtaylor@atlantic-pub.com
PROOFREADER: Angela Adams • aadams@atlantic-pub.com

Printed in the United States

We recently lost our beloved pet "Bear," who was not only our best and dearest friend but also the "Vice President of Sunshine" here at Atlantic Publishing. He did not receive a salary but worked tirelessly 24 hours a day to please his parents. Bear was a rescue dog that turned around and showered myself, my wife Sherri, his grandparents Jean, Bob and Nancy and every person and animal he met (maybe not rabbits) with friendship and love. He made a lot of people smile every day.

We wanted you to know that a portion of the profits of this book will be donated to The Humane Society of the United States.

–Douglas & Sherri Brown

THE HUMANE SOCIETY
OF THE UNITED STATES ©

The human-animal bond is as old as human history. We cherish our animal companions for their unconditional affection and acceptance. We feel a thrill when we glimpse wild creatures in their natural habitat or in our own backyard.

Unfortunately, the human-animal bond has at times been weakened. Humans have exploited some animal species to the point of extinction.

The Humane Society of the United States makes a difference in the lives of animals here at home and worldwide. The HSUS is dedicated to creating a world where our relationship with animals is guided by compassion. We seek a truly humane society in which animals are respected for their intrinsic value, and where the human-animal bond is strong.

Want to help animals? We have plenty of suggestions. Adopt a pet from a local shelter, join The Humane Society and be a part of our work to help companion animals and wildlife. You will be funding our educational, legislative, investigative and outreach projects in the U.S. and across the globe.

Or perhaps you'd like to make a memorial donation in honor of a pet, friend or relative? You can through our Kindred Spirits program. And if you'd like to contribute in a more structured way, our Planned Giving Office has suggestions about estate planning, annuities, and even gifts of stock that avoid capital gains taxes.

Maybe you have land that you would like to preserve as a lasting habitat for wildlife. Our Wildlife Land Trust can help you. Perhaps the land you want to share is a backyard—that's enough. Our Urban Wildlife Sanctuary Program will show you how to create a habitat for your wild neighbors.

So you see, it's easy to help animals. And The HSUS is here to help.

The Humane Society of the United States
2100 L Street NW
Washington, DC 20037
202-452-1100
www.hsus.org

Table of Contents

Preface

This book is written in the context of creating a guide for those students who wish to supplement their income while earning their degree. Whether you are looking for detailed information on the logistics of starting a business, weighing your options, creating a business from a current hobby, or you have finally decided to take that step into entrepreneurship, you will find all the information you need here.

Entrepreneurship is an exciting decision, but it is not all frosting. There is much to do — you will need to measure your ingredients just right (have the time and capital available), mix the ingredients together (write a business plan), bake for a little over an hour (it normally takes about a year to see an income from the business), wait for it to cool (inform the public it is all done), and then comes the frosting (you are earning your income).

The best part about owning your own business is that you are your own boss, and the worst part about owning your own business is you are the boss. Unless you own a partnership, you only have yourself to lean on, and only you can pick up extra shifts and make major decisions regarding the business. Do not worry — we have also covered the pros and cons of becoming a business owner, including information on where you can turn for help throughout every stage of your business. There are organizations and groups that you can join to gain support, and there are people who will offer business to business help, advice, and service trading.

How This Book Is Organized

This book is organized in a timeline format, detailing how to start and run any business. It is nearly a step-by-step process that offers everything you need to begin the development of your business. If you do not know what type of business you want to run, *101 Businesses You Can Start with Less Than One Thousand Dollars: For Students* offers information on the various businesses you can start from scratch with little or no money down.

The first section of the book is an overview that answers most of the questions you will have about starting a business and the concerns that surround it, including information about health care, retirement, and the pros and cons of running a business. In addition, you will learn numerous ways to test your business idea to see how well it will do in mainstream America.

The second section asks you to evaluate your decision to start your own business. Self-evaluation is an essential tool for the emerging entrepreneur, as it will help you assess the skills you have and offer information on developing those you lack. It is all right if you are not a whiz at accounting, finance, or other business-related aspects, but it is important to understand that they are needed to be successful in business. Taking a deeper look into your skills and assessing them properly will help realistically determine what type of business is right for you.

Deciding which business works best for you is not to be taken lightly. Your business will need to grow with you, meet your individual, financial, and family needs, and it must make you absolutely, positively happy. Running your own business can be a stressful situation at times, but doing something that makes you happy will relieve some of the stress. This section will help you choose the business that will complement your needs, have potential long-term benefits, and have the earning potential to fit your current needs.

Furthermore, the fourth section digs deep into the formation of any business structure and gives you a step-by-step guide to filing a business with your state, local government, and the IRS. It includes a discussion of business licenses, permits, and how to obtain them, if needed. The process may seem overwhelming but is in fact rather simple.

If you are not studying advertising the word can be scary and may make you want to run for the hills. However, everything you need to know about advertisement is laid out for your reading enjoyment. You will be shocked at how easy advertisement is.

A business plan is the most important material for growing a business; this is your business's calling card. Everyone you approach about your business will ask for this to-do list. And you cannot do anything without it. Need some startup money? Need to approach investors? Need to outsource or file government paperwork? You will hear the same thing every time: "Do you have a business plan?" The process may seem a little lengthy, but having one is paramount to your business's success. Think of it as an extremely detailed to-do list. We have detailed the outline for writing your business plan and included tips on preparing it. For many entrepreneurs this is the reason their business has had continued success.

Here comes the tricky part — finding ways to finance your business. Financing can be the most important part of getting your business up and running, introducing it to the public, or expanding it when it grows. You might already have the capital and equipment to start your business, but when your business begins to grow keep this section handy. You might need it down the road.

Introduction

Almost any hobby you have ever done, any service you have ever provided, or any job you may have succeeded at in the past can be your own business. My first successful business was just that—a hobby. I produced a gift for a family member, and from there grew a digital scrap booking business I called "Magic Memories." That business became a full-slated production company that included school graduation clients and expanded into a product for the entire student body.

Any job you have performed for another business or individual can be done on your own. My second successful business was put together after my husband's company went bankrupt. Without his income our financial stability was a tad shaky. He went out on his own, and his business has become larger than we would have ever expected. His clientele from his previous company followed him to his new, self-owned business, and today he continues to offer his services, while I market, advertise, and provide the administrative work.

There are those people who start a business without even thinking they have started one. They simply began offering their service or got talked into doing it for someone, and suddenly they are making money. How many of us had a lemonade stand? Offered to rake leaves for a neighbor? Baby sat a neighbor's kids?

Throughout the pages of this book we have compiled case studies of successful business owners, businesses you can start for under $1,000, and detailed information on how to start, expand, and run any home-based business. We have provided infinite hours of research and profiles of successful individuals for your learning enjoyment. The only thing we left out was the decision to make it happen and the desire to work for yourself; these things are left up to you.

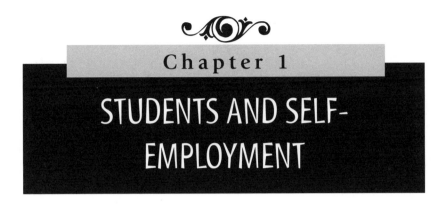

Chapter 1

STUDENTS AND SELF-EMPLOYMENT

"Real success is finding your lifework in the work that you love."

-David McCullough

Starting a business is not for a select group of people, privileged individuals, or only adults. You do not have to come from a family who previously owned a business, nor do you have to have a business degree or any degree yet at all. Anyone who has devotion and drive, a passion for success, and an understanding of business concepts can run a business.

If you have no idea what type of business you would like to run, we have provided you with detailed information on over 100 businesses that have a history of success. We have found a way to make it easy for students to find that perfect income before earning their degree.

Are You Up for Self-Employment?

Self-employment is not for everyone; you will have to decide if self-employment is the best thing for you. It is important to get feedback from your family and those closest to you. Allow them to address the concerns and thoughts they may have about your venture. Building a business takes a lot of dedication in the first year.

Considering your current role as a student, what do you specifically think you would gain from starting your own business? While starting your own business offers many advantages, as a student there are some very specific advantages to starting a business, including:

- **Financial Freedom** – When you work for someone else you get paid only for the time you actually work. When you work for yourself, you make money 24 hours a day, 7 days a week, especially if you are selling on the Web.

- **Flexible Hours** – When you work for yourself you have the advantage of creating a schedule that can change as necessary so you can maintain your current school schedule. You can work more during breaks and take time off for exam week.

- **Your Time, Your Training** – When you work for yourself, you decide what is important for you to know. You will earn hands on training in a variety of subjects. In a corporate job you would be limited to one job and one set of duties and responsibilities.

- **Responsibility** – As your own boss, you are responsible for the successes or disappointments you face. As it stands right now, if you are working for someone else, you are giving that person entire control over your situation. By taking control of your future, you have no one to blame but yourself for your difficulties. On the other hand, you have no one to praise but yourself when you create a successful and marketable business.

- **Experience** – Owning your own business will give you the experience you need to succeed in any endeavor in the future, even if your business fails.

We have dedicated an entire chapter to self-evaluation so you can gain some insight into your personal and professional characteristics and to help you figure out the right business and the right process to take for starting your business.

The Challenges of Starting a Business as a Student

The one major challenge that young entrepreneurs face is finding the capital and obtaining a loan to start a home-based or small business. The age of the loan seeker is an extremely important factor for lenders. Most will not give a loan to a young entrepreneur; however, there are lenders who feel that young entrepreneurs have a more vital spirit and can make a larger return. It is an evident road block students will face when they attempt to get loans.

Young entrepreneurs work fewer hours, take more vacations, and tend not to have any employees. They also have the freedom to perform a job at their own pace and on their own schedule, all characteristics that indicate their business will be successful.

The Pros and Cons of Self-Employment

Of course, everything has a good side and bad side. That is life. There was no way we could create this book without looking at the pros and the cons to help you make a well-informed decision.

Pros	Cons
You are your own boss	You will only have yourself to lean on
You will know exactly where your money is going	The first year there will be no steady income

Tax breaks and tax benefits	You have to do your own accounting
More freedom with your schedule	You have to set your own schedule and keep everything in line
You gain more personal exposure by selling for yourself	No regular health insurance

Personal Pros and Cons

Now that we have given you an example of some of the pros and cons, it is time for you to give this exercise a try. Write down your own personal pros and cons in regard to starting and running your own business.

Failure Rates of Small Businesses

GardenerBusiness.com states that businesses fail at 90 percent rate in their first year of operation. This is a staggering figure if you are looking to start your own business. If you look at it from almost any perspective, that number will give you doubts about putting your time and effort into starting a business.

You do not have to be alarmed by that statistic. Instead, be aware that you are starting out fresh and with one of the best tools behind you, *101 Businesses You Can Start for Less Than One Thousand Dollars: For Students.*

There are a number of reasons why companies fail. One of the biggest reasons that small businesses fail is an inadequate or not thought out business plan, which is why we have included a chapter on business plans. Business plans are to a business owner like navigational systems are to a ship captain. It is the one thing that will keep you from crashing into business wasteland.

Let us take a look at some of the top reasons why businesses fail:

- Not a defined enough business plan

- Money runs out before the business can start its earnings

- Inadequate business management

- Business owners get discouraged

- The health of the owners

- Obligations unforeseen by the owner

The one thing that needs to be emphasized in this chapter is that you should learn everything you can about starting and running and maintaining a business, before you think of anything else. To make it successful you need to dot your i's and cross your t's.

Why Is It That Businesses Are Successful?

Business owners should believe in themselves and their product/service, first and foremost. Making money should not be their primary motivation, but instead what inspires them is providing a service/product that they believe in to the public. And most important successful business owners do not give up when things start to get tough; they stick to it and propel through with full force.

If you set your sights on owning and running a small business, do not let anyone tell you no or that you cannot do it. Take some very famous pioneers of our time for example: Dr. Seuss, the renowned and much loved children's book author, was rejected more than 27 times when he sent his first children's book out for publication. Now we need to get you going on your way to entrepreneurship.

10 Reasons You Should Start a Business

We all need a little push now and then to get started toward our goals and dreams. Although we want to be honest about the obstacles you will be facing while starting, running, and maintaining your business, we also want to outline the benefits. We have put together a list of the top ten reasons why you should get started turning your business into reality:

1. Living your dreams

2. Having the flexibility to work, maintain your school schedule, and schedule other things

3. The initial investment is low

4. You decide everything

5. No commute — save on gas

6. You have time for family and other hobbies

7. You are spending your time doing something you love

8. Having the extra money for personal expenses

9. Can help you pay for school

10. Have something to brag about on your résumé

Test Your Idea

After you have decided to go into business for yourself and before you begin creating the business from scratch, a good plan would be to first test your business concept. There are a few different ways you can do this:

1. Get in touch with family and friends

2. Create a mail marketing questionnaire

3. Contact potential customers

4. Ask strangers

Your family and friends can offer great insight into whether your business idea will work. Knowing them on a personal level will make it easier for you to explain your concept and how you plan to make your business idea happen. They may be able to add some favorable insight into what would make your business better or more marketable. You can also ask your teachers or professors for their thoughts on your business idea.

When you do address your family and friends you want to be in a casual setting. Ask them about the business as you would ask how your outfit looks on you, subtle but serious. Sometimes it is nice to get some of your most important questions answered like:

1. How well will the public like/need my product or service?

2. What percentage of the community would use/want/need my product or service?

3. Who would most use/buy my product or service?

4. How much would individuals be willing to spend on my product or service?

5. How many times a year will my product or service be in demand?

6. How can I make this a product or service my customers will need many times throughout the year?

7. Which income bracket are my clients in?

8. Where will they most likely buy this product: online, in a store, at the mall, and so on?

With a postcard mailing you might not get all the questions you want answered, but you can get the most important ones answered.

If you are interested in putting together a postcard questionnaire, in which potential customers or community members would answer the questions and send it back to you, contact your local office store (Kinkos, Staples, Office Depot, Office Max, and so on) and ask about putting something together. Whether you send out a flyer or a postcard, be sure to include the postage for the client to send the questionnaires back to you.

You can obtain mailing list information from an organization that provides lists by category, such as Lists Are Us (**www.listsareus.com**) or USA Data (**www.usadata.com**). You can expect one out of every ten to come back to you. Therefore, if you need around 100 responses, you should send out at least 1,000.

Potential clients could be a helpful tool for setting up your business. If your potential clients are small business owners', contact some in your area, and explain your intention for your business; how you plan to better assist them, how your service/product is different than the competition's, and how you can save them money in that area. Their advice and enthusiasm for your idea can help you better determine and adjust your business plan.

Strangers are unbiased bystanders. Screenwriters are known to ask people in line at a grocery store or gas station if they would be interested in seeing a movie about their idea. Some may be honest and helpful; others may not want to be bothered, but there is the potential to garner some opinions. Although some people may not be as enthusiastic as you, surveying random people is a helpful option to explore.

Organizations You Can Turn to for Help

You will find a number of organizations available to help you obtain your dream. Whether through the net or local office branches in your community, there are a number of organizations that will help you start a business, polish or review your business plan, advise you on obtaining financial assistance and support, and give you information on running or expanding your business.

Online

Small Business Resources — A site written by and for entrepreneurs who share their first-hand knowledge of how to succeed in small business. Free, helpful advice from small business and Internet experts. (**www.smallbusinessresources.com**)

The IRS — Small Business Resources provided by the IRS. Tons of information for the small business owner as well as up-to-date information about tax incentives and new programs for the small business. This site also offers free software to the small business owner. (**www.irs.gov**)

The United States Small Business Administration — The small Business Administration is another government ran Web portal with business planners, tools, resources, and articles for the small business owner. (**www.sba.gov**)

All Business — All Business provides articles with advice for small business owners, as well as a selection of common forms and various resources and links. (**www.allbusiness.com**)

Health Care and Retirement for the Self-employed

Health care can be a major expense, especially when you are on your own. Here are some options for those just getting their business off the ground to consider.

First. You can get free health care through your counties jobs and family service center. Your local jobs and family service centers can give you and your family full coverage insurance depending on how much your current family income is. You should contact your local jobs and family service center to find out how to apply and to see if you are eligible for this practical benefit.

Second. You can locate a health clinic that accepts payment on a sliding scale. There are a number of clinics that use a sliding scale for the use of their services. They take into account your current income and adjust it to how much you can afford to pay. This could come out to you paying anywhere from 0 to 100 percent. Normally these clinics are found in your local phone book. This also applies to many clinical dentist offices as well.

Third. You can become a member of low cost health care options with your state or local government. You can contact your local health department to obtain information on local government or national government programs for working families. The benefits are unlimited and include complete dental, medical, eye, and prescription services for a low fee. Eligibility depends on your family size and current income ratio.

Fourth. Membership groups, such as small business and the type of industry you are affiliated with (writers, media and so on) all offer their members low cost health insurance.

One thing many hospitals do not always disclose is that you can also receive emergency visits on a sliding scale fee. If you have an emergency visit or are forced to have unforeseen surgery and are currently without health care, you can ask for an H-CAP application. How much you pay will be on a family size to current income ratio. This program will/could almost pay off the entire hospital bill.

SUCCESS STORY: LAKESHORE ACADEMY OF FINE ARTS

Sarah Ilijanich started her business, Lakeshore Academy of Fine Arts, in September of 1998. She offers after school programs to students in the fine arts. "I started it because I was young, full of ambition, and lacked the common sense that comes with age and experience," says Mrs. Ilijanich.

Her business	We enrich young minds into innovative thinking through the medium of fine arts. The school provides training in theatre and drama, also assisting children in audition pieces when acquiring a talent agent, magazine modeling, TV commercial callbacks, and other such acting devices.
How her idea was sparked	I taught acting classes in an after school program at a private school for three years. During this time, the number of students grew considerably and I had several private students I was tutoring. I had an itch to direct Wizard of Oz. However, the private school would not fund a 'superfluous' performance. So, I sought out funding elsewhere. It was a tremendous success, and Lakeshore Academy of Fine Arts was founded shortly after.
Why she started her own business	Starting my own business came from within, but the support of my husband, Steve, and my parents made it possible. Being very passionate about acting and the benefits one can gain from such a theatrical experience made it easy to dream. Honestly, belief is the key. Believing is the art of innovation. If you cannot envision your dream, it will not become anything.
The pros and cons	Advantage: Control – it's your baby.
	Disadvantage: Control – Learning to trust others.
Type of business	I did have a storefront for a few years. Now I privately tutor, direct performances, and perform presentations. I am also writing fictional children's books.
Concerns when starting her business	Money! You win some, you lose some. It's a little like gambling. It's a risk to find out what people want and don't want.

SUCCESS STORY: LAKESHORE ACADEMY OF FINE ARTS	
How she overcame her concerns	Theatre moms and dads are very opinionated, and so was I. I had to learn to work with them instead of at them. It's a delicate thing – teaching children and being young can distract parents from trusting your experiences. Having 11 years under my belt and waiting lists has alleviated this somewhat.
Saw a steady flow of income...	In 2 years.
Her likes and dislikes about running a business	I love teaching. Watching kids develop into confident beings is very rewarding. They change right before your eyes, in the process of putting on a performance. Trying to balance your passionate ideas can be frustrating.
Future aspirations for her business	As my own children grow older, the school will open its doors to all the arts. Dance, music, creative writing, film, yoga, and so on.
Her personal qualities that have helped her in her business endeavors	I am a highly innovative individual with extensive analytical qualities. I can read people. I know how to get what I want. If I don't, I research it until I find out. Persistence to bulldoze yourself through the slush. I needed to self-motivate, self-congratulate, and self-direct myself. No one is going to help pick you up if you fail to help yourself.
The key to her success	When I lacked confidence I faked it. No one seeks knowledge from someone who doesn't believe in what they are saying. What if the Wicked Witch of the West knew she would die in the end? Would she keep trying to get those ruby slippers? Where would the story be then? No one is going to sit watching a play about a witch sitting on her tush waiting for the slippers to come her way. If you want something, stop worrying about the consequences and go get it. When someone knocks you down, get back up. Unless that is – you just don't want it that bad. Taking a risk is about rewards and consequences. You have to weigh them and decide if it's worth it.

SUCCESS STORY: LAKESHORE ACADEMY OF FINE ARTS	
A challenge she faced while running her business	I was challenged when I took on too many jobs at once. I was running a big performance of West Side Story, and I had encountered a mental block. I didn't trust anyone to anything. I was the set designer, the stage manager, the director, the dance instructor, and so on. I learned to bite my tongue and trust in others. Sometimes you butt heads, but I learned to compromise and listen.
Advice to new business owners	Do it. What is the true risk? You fail. Oh well, there's always tomorrow.
The ease of breaking into her industry	It's only hard if you don't believe in what you are doing. This world is built around vibes. Give the client what they want. If you're not the right guy for the job, send them elsewhere. They will respect you for it. Don't give someone a product they don't want. They will remember how they felt.
How she was able to start her business	I was lucky my husband had a good job and provided our family with what we needed. But a business takes money to run. So, I waited tables, babysat, waited tables some more, and even worked at the local gym to keep it moving along.
The importance of a support group to her	You need to seek refuge and advice from everything and everyone. God, family, friends, nature; it doesn't matter as long as it gets you past the 'blocks.'
The challenges she has faced	What challenges haven't I faced? Instead of looking at problems as a negative, I looked at them as an opportunity to problem solve. In acting, there is a tool we use called a GOTE sheet. I apply it to life constantly. G – Goals (identify long term and short term). Ex. I want to take over the world. I need to invade Germany, then Mexico, etc and so on. O – Obstacles (identify mental, physical, & and environmental). Ex. I don't know enough about battle fighting, I have a bad heart, and there is a hailstorm coming.

SUCCESS STORY: LAKESHORE ACADEMY OF FINE ARTS	
	T – Tactics (identify positive and negative). Ex. In taking over the world I can use a threatening tactic or I can bribe them.
	E – Expectation (it is always your long- term goal). Ex. I expect to take over the world!
What it takes to be successful in business	Guts! Passion, persistence, and desire.
When she knew her business was a success	I stopped teaching for a year and people still kept calling to see when my next class was.
Her most bizarre request	Someone asked me to make their daughter Britney Spears. She was 5.

Chapter 2

Self-Evaluation

Self-evaluation is an important step that should be done before you push forward on your venture of entrepreneurship. As stated in the last chapter, one of the biggest reasons small businesses fail is because the owner did not take the necessary steps for self-evaluation and business planning.

What if you believe you are not ready to start a home business after you complete the self-evaluation process? Do not fret. If you have enough capital, you can hire others to help in the areas you lack. If you do not, you can always take some classes or workshops to brush up on the necessary subject.

The Importance of Being Earnest

No matter what you plan to do with your future being earnest is an important part of beginning the journey. And having your own business is nothing but getting yourself on the path of productivity. So let us get started on making ourselves ready for business. Let us start with your strengths and weaknesses.

Place a check mark in the box of each sub-field of sales that you believe you can accomplish at a rate of 90 percent accuracy.

IN WHICH AREAS OF SALES DO YOU HAVE AN ABOVE-AVERAGE KNOWLEDGE?

- ☐ **Value** – Can you price your services or products accurately?
- ☐ **Purchasing** – Can you find the best value for your dollar?
- ☐ **Negotiations** – Can you negotiate in pricing or purchasing?
- ☐ **Competitor Analysis** – Can you compare and rate competitors in your area?
- ☐ **Direct Sales** – Can you directly sell to a client?
- ☐ **Sales Planning** – Can you competitively plan for the sales and buying that will make up sales in your business?

How Did You Score?

If you marked four or more boxes – awesome. You have great sales knowledge, and you should move on to the next category. If you marked three of the boxes – that is good. It would be a good idea to brush up on the sub-fields that you did not check so you have a better understanding of sales. If you marked three or less – do not worry. You can take an online course, pick up a book, or take a workshop to improve your skills.

IN WHICH AREAS OF MARKETING DO YOU HAVE ABOVE-AVERAGE KNOWLEDGE?

- ☐ **Advertising** – Do you understand the mechanics of advertising?
- ☐ **Public Relations** – Do you know what public relations takes to succeed?
- ☐ **Promotions** – Can you provide quick and cost-effective promotional campaigns?
- ☐ **Media Relations** – Do you know how to gain access to the media?
- ☐ **Marketing Strategies** – Can you come up with brilliant new ways to make your service/product a household name?
- ☐ **Annual Marketing Plans** – Can you provide an outline of a year's worth of marketing for your business?

How Did You Score?

If you marked four or more boxes – Yeah! You will have a marketing plan to end all others. If you marked three of the boxes – Super. But it would be a good idea to brush up on the sub-fields that you did not check so you have a better overall understanding. If you marked three or less – No worries. You can take an online course, pick up a book, or take a workshop to improve your skills.

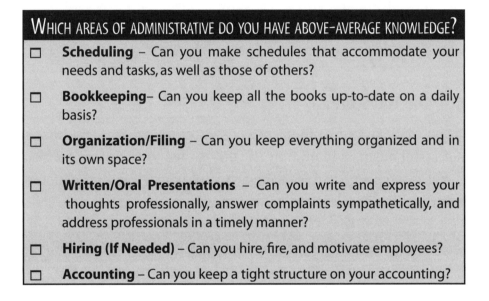

WHICH AREAS OF ADMINISTRATIVE DO YOU HAVE ABOVE–AVERAGE KNOWLEDGE?

☐ **Scheduling** – Can you make schedules that accommodate your needs and tasks, as well as those of others?

☐ **Bookkeeping**– Can you keep all the books up-to-date on a daily basis?

☐ **Organization/Filing** – Can you keep everything organized and in its own space?

☐ **Written/Oral Presentations** – Can you write and express your thoughts professionally, answer complaints sympathetically, and address professionals in a timely manner?

☐ **Hiring (If Needed)** – Can you hire, fire, and motivate employees?

☐ **Accounting** – Can you keep a tight structure on your accounting?

How Did You Score?

If you marked four or more boxes – Tremendous. You are well on your way to running a successful business. If you marked three of the boxes – That is terrific. It would be great for you to refresh yourself on the sub-fields that you did not check. If you marked three or less – Do not be concerned. You can take an online course, pick up a book, or take a workshop to improve your skills.

IN WHICH AREAS OF FINANCIAL MANAGEMENT DO YOU HAVE AN ABOVE-AVERAGE KNOWLEDGE?

- ☐ **Credit/loan Lines** – Can you keep and maintain lines of credit?
- ☐ **Monthly Finances** – Can you read, produce, and keep up-to-date monthly finances?
- ☐ **Bank Relations** – Can you negotiate on the various aspects of bank relations?
- ☐ **Billing** – Can you keep accounts of and produce invoices and information for billing customers?
- ☐ **Tax Preparation** – Can you prepare tax forms accurately?
- ☐ **Balance Sheets** – Can you maintain balance sheets?

How Did You Score?

If you marked four or more boxes – Astounding. You will have a successful business in no time. If you marked three or less – Super. It still may be a good idea to re-acquaint yourself with those sub-fields with a course, book, or workshop.

WHICH CHARACTERISTICS DO YOU FEEL YOU POSSESS?

- ☐ You can work long hours and not be alarmed.
- ☐ You can handle and work under stress.
- ☐ You have tons of family support.
- ☐ You understand that you may stumble a lot in your first year or two, but you are prepared to see those stumbles as stepping-stones.
- ☐ You are able to work with clients and employees in a polite and professional manner.
- ☐ You are able to work alone.

How Did You Score?

If you marked four or more boxes – Wow, you are good. You have the characteristics of a true entrepreneur. If you marked three or less – It is all right. You can take an online course, pick up a book, or take a workshop.

How Much Do You Need to Earn?

Let us now take a look at one of the most important questions: How much do you need to earn? What you want to earn and what you need to earn are two different things. Fill in the chart below to make an accurate account of your household and business expenses. These should be accurate estimations of what your expenses will look like in the next year. Only fill in those which you pay.

	HOUSEHOLD EXPENSES	BUSINESS EXPENSES
Mortgage/Rent		
Electricity		
Phone		
Cable		
Internet		
Loans		
Credit cards		
Professional fees		
Supplies		
Food		
Insurance		
Unexpected expenses		
Total budget going out		
Tax		
Grand total		
Add both totals together		

Now that you have a grand total, this will give you a better idea of what you will to need to earn. Although there are some businesses that will only allow you to break even in the first year, there are some that will give you a return right away.

Startup Fees

Let us look at some additional charges you may endure for the business startup. In some businesses this will be an outrageous amount, especially if you need to use a storefront and you need extra help from outside sources, such as financial institutions or family and friends.

	OVERHEAD EXPENSES
Storage or additional spacing	
Building/Design	
Advertisement	
Security	
Professional fees	
Supplies	
Deposits	
Startup inventory	
Insurance	
Miscellaneous	
Total budget going out	
Tax	
Grand total	

Business Idea Evaluation

If you have not decided which business is suited best for you or which business you would like to be involved in for the next ten years, fill out the business idea evaluation form to help you choose the perfect business for your personal, family, and happiness needs. It is suggested that you pick at least three or four businesses that you would personally enjoy doing to evaluate which one will be best for you.

BUSINESS IDEA ONE

	Yes	No
Is this a business you could do for the next 10 years?		
Do you have at least three years of experience in this field?		
Is this a business that is easy to break into?		
Does the earning potential exceed your family budget?		
Does this business have good market value?		
Do you have a variety of ways to make the product/service unique or different?		
Do you understand the core concept of producing this service/product?		
Have you ever worked in this field before?		
Do you get excited about the business?		
Can the capital you currently have take care of the startup costs for this business?		
Can running this business work well with your family needs?		
Does this business give you more freedom?		
Does this business have growth potential for the future?		
Add the yes and no columns individually		

BUSINESS IDEA TWO

	Yes	No
Is this a business you could do for the next 10 years?		
Do you have at least three years of experience in this field?		
Is this a business that is easy to break into?		
Does the earning potential exceed your family budget?		
Does this business have good market value?		
Do you have a variety of ways to make the product/service unique or different?		

	Yes	No
Do you understand the core concept of producing this service/product?		
Have you ever worked in this field before?		
Do you get excited about the business?		
Can the capital you currently have take care of the startup costs for this business?		
Can running this business work well with your family needs?		
Does this business give you more freedom?		
Does this business have growth potential for the future?		
Add the yes and no columns individually		

BUSINESS IDEA THREE		
	Yes	No
Is this a business you could do for the next 10 years?		
Do you have at least three years of experience in this field?		
Is this a business that is easy to break into?		
Does the earning potential exceed your family budget?		
Does this business have good market value?		
Do you have a variety of ways to make the product/service unique or different?		
Do you understand the core concept of producing this service/product?		
Have you ever worked in this field before?		
Do you get excited about the business?		
Can the capital you currently have take care of the startup costs for this business?		
Can running this business work well with your family needs?		
Does this business give you more freedom?		
Does this business have future growth potential?		
Add the yes and no columns individually		

The business idea with the most yes answers will be a great business for you. If you have more than three business ideas to consider, redo the evaluation form, eliminating the ones with the most no's, until you have three top choices. Then use the business evaluation form just one more time.

When you finally have your top choice, get out there and get your business rolling.

Checklist for Starting Your Business

The following checklist does not only apply to this chapter; you can use this throughout your startup year.

THE GROUND WORK
☐ Acquire the perfect business for you.
☐ Assess the startup costs.
☐ Determine your goals (both personal and business).
☐ Determine financial resources.
☐ Establish a marketing plan.
☐ Identify your potential customers.
☐ Research your competition.
☐ Write a business plan.
☐ Choose your business name.

THE STARTUP
☐ Establish your home office.
☐ Set up a business account
☐ File for an employee identification number (this is used like your business's social security number).
☐ Register the business with your state.
☐ Incorporate your business.
☐ Obtain licensing (if needed).
☐ Obtain insurance (if needed).
☐ Hire professionals in the areas you need help in.

THE OPENING	
☐ Set an opening date.	☐ Acquire necessary inventory.
☐ Plan an opening celebration.	☐ Join a professional group or organization.
☐ Advertise.	
☐ Get business cards.	☐ Purchase signs.

Know Your Current Market

Your market is the primary individuals — according to geography, gender, age, or profession — who will be your target audience. But who are they, what are their likes, how do they make their buying decisions, and so forth?

MARKET EVALUATION FORM

1. Explain your business idea: _____
    _____.

2. How will this service/product be used? _____
    _____.

3. Are there local products/services in your area similar to yours? _____
    _____.

4. How does yours differ? What is the unique angle? _____
    _____.

5. Where do your prospective clients live? _____
    _____.

6. What type of entertainment do your potential clients seek? _____
    _____.

7. Where do your potential clients shop? _____
    _____.

8. What are the newspapers, magazines, newsletters that your prospective clients read? _____
    _____.

9. What TV and radio stations do your prospective clients watch and listen to? _____
    _____.

Putting It All Together

Now it is time for you to put all your planning into action. The last few chapters are set up to help you put everything together and make your dream a reality.

SUCCESS STORY: HAPPY VALLEY NOTARY

JoAnne Davis started her business, Happy Valley Notary, in California. She said, "I would never go back to working for someone else." She started her personal service business in 2004 to offer a number of services to the community.

"I was an in home care provider for mentally retarded adults. I stopped working when my oldest brother became so ill we thought we were going to lose him. My mother's health was failing at the same time, and when she almost died, I quit work to help them both," said JoAnne. Read about her and her business and visit her on the Web at **www.happyvalley.com**.

Her business	We offer many services from one small location, like a notary. Our services are geared toward helping our small community with many "Free or No Charge" items.
How her idea was sparked	Family history supplied the means of being business minded, starting with my mother who was a very intelligent woman. She started her own pet store within two weeks of having the idea. On her passing and my becoming an ordained minister through online channels, a friend asked me to honor them by performing their wedding. It turned out to be a beautiful ceremony, and I've been hooked ever since.
Why she started her own business	My own personal grief led me to become an ordained minister in the hopes of learning more about how to handle the five stages of grief we all go through at the loss of a loved one. In the need to better myself I started studying many things both online and off. Becoming a notary public was my first thing to accomplish. Since then I have learned and become certified in many things. Opening a small office to offer this knowledge seemed the only logical thing to do after that.

SUCCESS STORY: HAPPY VALLEY NOTARY	
The pros and cons	PRO: You can do it from your home, a small office, and take it mobile. You don't have to be tied down to one certain place. You can make appointments to travel. If you need to step away, or have a time when you simply don't wish to work that day for whatever reason, you can do so without a great loss. Simply manage your time around that day.
	CON: Personal service customers tend to be more aggressive in their attitudes toward a notary public. They expect you to know exactly what they need, how it should be worded, which we are not allowed by state law to do. We are not lawyers or legal aide. We notarize signatures on documents, such as loans, applications, etc. If they do not know what they need and you tell them that you can't provide the answer, many aren't happy.
Type of business	I felt it best at the time to set up the business as sole proprietor due to the simple fact my husband said it was "my baby" and other than help with moving heavy things, he wouldn't be able to do much more since he is only home one day a week. I alone have to answer for anything in the company.
She saw a steady flow of income in...	I'm not sure if I still have a steady flow. It all depends on how hard you work at building up the business, what your goals are, what your overhead and operating costs are. Since I've always done this from home, until recently when I moved into a small mobile office my overhead was next to nothing. The harder you work, the more you put your self out there, let others know who you are and what you can do for them, the better your business will be. Don't expect any kind of return on your small investment for at least a year. This is the kind of business with a small startup, but it still takes time to get known.

SUCCESS STORY: HAPPY VALLEY NOTARY	
Her likes and dislikes about running a business	LIKES: The glow on the couples' faces when I announce them husband and wife. The sheer happiness that surrounds you when you've done well and others acknowledge it. When you see the tears form, in eyes that glow from happiness, and the ceremony is so touching. That's why I do it.
	DISLIKES: The rudeness of any kind and when you're in the public eye so to speak you are subject to all kinds of rudeness. People get loud, rude, don't always use common sense, and hold you personally responsible for every detail and can be really rude about it. On the special day of a wedding many things can go wrong, that's why you pay attention to details; have your checklists to ensure a perfect day.
Future aspirations for her business	One can never foretell the future; we can only accept and work toward what we wish it to be. I would like to think my future holds many more weddings, successful dealings with the public. To bring the business up to a level of competency I would expect from another. Perhaps to bring in a cash flow that would allow me to maintain the ability to help my children if they needed me. To be able to open my arms to all that need a hug. My dream was to open a soup kitchen, so to speak; perhaps one day I may be able to.
Her personal qualities that have helped her in her business endeavors	I am stubborn and refuse to back down. I am not a quitter and refuse to give up when the going gets harder than what I may be used to. My loving nature, the ability to listen, pay attention to details, and the strangest craving for knowledge.
The key to her success	I live by a quote: "The only time success comes before work is in the dictionary."
	Hard work, understanding, patience, and the willingness to learn all that I can about my business. Taking a risk is about rewards and consequences. You have to weigh them and decide if it's worth it.

SUCCESS STORY: HAPPY VALLEY NOTARY

A challenge she faced while running her business	Every time I have to stand up in front of people is a challenge for me since I am basically very shy. Over coming my small stuttering has been the hardest challenge to date. I need to be clear and concise, which I strive to do. When I first opened the mobile office I was so happy and everything was falling into place the way it should. All details I thought were in place until I realized that where I was going to be located only had dial up for my online needs. I called every single provider I could find online and in the local area, not one provided DSL or cable at my new location. They supplied DSL to the address next door, but not where I was. So I settled for dial up until I realized my old laptop would not work on dial up service it was so slow. Once it took ten minutes for a page to load. I've had a few customers for U-Haul walk out because they didn't want to wait any longer. I even bought a new PC and that didn't help. The office being a small mobile wasn't permitted to be close to the electrical outlets I needed so I have to run a 100 foot cord twice a day just to have the power to operate the PC and printer. Sprint.com now has a wireless broadband card for desktops; I just received it today and I am hoping that will help the Internet speed! The electrical, well, I need the exercise!
Her advice to potential business owners	Have tons of patience, be willing to work hard, learn all you can about the business you wish to start. Folks have this uncanny way of asking the oddest questions and when you can give them an answer, you've got their business! Take a few classes in public speaking, accounting, and time to learn. Just as you make a business plan to help you know what you need, the research, targets and so forth, have a "back out" plan. Give yourself the okay to stop putting out money on something that may truly not be working. Give yourself a deadline to make or break and stick to it. It's not quitting or giving up; it's making a good sound financial decision.

SUCCESS STORY: HAPPY VALLEY NOTARY

The ease of breaking into her industry	I personally think it's easy to do. If you have the gift of gab, the loving nature, the strong sense of helping others, the financial means, and the willingness to work, yes, it is easy.
Her Business Day	I work eight hour days, six days a week. Sunday is my time with my family, but I still make appointments if the person really needs me that day. I own the business and can do as I please. If I don't wish to work that day I put a notice on the door stating I will be closed for personal reasons, and if it's a emergency, call me at home. So far in the small community it hasn't bothered the business at all.
What it takes to be successful in business	"The only time success comes before work is in the dictionary." Learn it, live by it, and work hard at it.
She knew her business was a success	My youngest brother Paul asked me to marry him to his now wife Lyndy; if he trusted me, then the public could.
Her most bizarre request	To do a hand fasting sky clad, which simply means nude. At my age of 51, there's not a chance that will ever happen. Since I also do alternative weddings, like same sex ceremonies, hand fasting, jumping the broom, I'm never sure what I may be asked to do. Theme weddings are wonderful especially if you like to get dressed up in costumes!
Her most embarrassing moment	My very first wedding when my knees were shaking in total fear and my back problems jumped up the day before the ceremony was to take place. I couldn't back out at the last minute so I took a handful of ibuprofens to help with the pain. I was so nervous that I felt like I was going to fall, but my daughter said she couldn't tell at all!

Chapter 3

Businesses You Can Start For Between $0 And $100

"Everyone has a talent; what is rare is the courage to follow the talent to the dark place where it leads."

-Erica Jong

Where to Start Freelancing

If you will be offering services as a freelancer, you can bid on jobs today to start working tomorrow. You can become involved in any one of the following businesses or industries:

- Writing
- Research
- ,Editing
- Logo design
- Web design

- Graphic design
- Marketing – advertising – sales
- Database creation and maintaining
- Business consulting

- Photography – videography
- Administrative assistants
- Accounting – finances

You can find hundreds of well paying jobs through these, and other, freelance job sites:

- www.project4hire.com
- www.findwebdesigners.net
- www.ifreelance.com
- www.sologig.com
- www.gofreelance.com
- www.guru.com

Some Web sites charge a monthly membership fee or a per project fee, but the sites and jobs are legitimate, paying jobs. These freelance jobs may start as a jumping off point. Perhaps you can use the jobs you complete here as references or referrals once you become established. Besides, you can start making money in a day.

How to Read Each Profile

The following business ideas are coordinated to help you easily understand how it works, the basic skills needed to complete the tasks, how to provide the service, how to start offering the services, ideas on creative ways to get your name and your company's name in the spotlight, possible income, and your initial clientele. You will also find information about organizations, groups, and places to turn to for help and where to go to obtain clients. This information should give you a better outlook and understanding of the task at hand and which type of business would work best for you.

The symbols are used for ease of viewing the potential money, business equipment, business base, if there are other businesses you can coordinate with, and clientele in each business idea. If you want to glance through the ideas, this will make it easier to see which has the highest yearly profit, needs the most equipment, if there will be travel time, or how large of a clientele you potentially have.

THE SYMBOLS

The ★ symbol rates the business in general: its potential earnings, ease of breaking in, the at-home time compared to travel, and the potential for future growth. ★ Not the greatest ★ ★ ★ ★ ★ ★ ★ ★ ★ The best ever	The $ symbol indicates the potential yearly income. $ Up to $20,000 $$ $20,000 - $60,000 $$$ $60,000 - $100,000 $$$$ Over $100,000
The ease of breaking into the business. 🔓 This is easy to break into 🔒 This business is hard to break into, although you do have a good opportunity to work in this field, it tends to be hard in the beginning stages.	The symbols indicate the potential clientele. 💬 A select group 💬 Local clients only 💬 The world
The following symbols are used for the business equipment section. They indicate which office equipment you need to get started. 📱 Cell phone 📠 Fax 📄 Printer ☎ Landline Phone 🖥 Computer 🗄 Inventory 💿 Software	The following symbols provide the information for your home base. 🏪 The business should have a storefront or will be conducted in an office or other people's homes. 🏠 This is merely an at-home business. 🚗 This business requires travel time. 🌐 This is an Internet business
* If you see this symbol * in the business overview section, it means there is another business you could conduct, along with this particular business, to make extra money.	

So let us take a look at how the business ideas are put together for you.

The Business ✫ ✫ ✫

Business Overview:

This section will go over the basic concept of the idea, what your primary job duties will be, and other tips about the business idea.

Show Me the Money: $$$

This section was developed to give you detailed information on how much you may need to start the business, how much to charge, and about how long it will take to see an income.

Business Equipment: 📱 ☎ 🖥 📄

Under the business equipment section you will find additional equipment that you may need besides the common equipment in every home office in America, which should include: a basic computer system set up with a printer/fax/copier, paper and accessories, a cell phone, and a landline phone that is set up for business purposes only. Another addition to your business equipment should be business cards; these should be printed from a specialty printing shop and handed out to any and every contact you make.

Business Base: 🏠 🏔

Is this a strictly at-home business or will there need to be a storefront? How much travel time does this business entail? All these questions will be answered in the business base section of the idea.

Clientele: 🗣 💬

Provided in this section will be the majority of the clientele you should be seeking and creative clientele you may have never thought of.

Starting Point: 🔓

How do you get started? This section details the steps to get the business up and running. It also provides marketing and promotional tips to help get the word out about your business.

Learn More:

If you want more information about the particular idea, this section will provide it, including Web sites, organizations, and affiliate groups that can help you gain more knowledge regarding the business idea.

The core information provided for each of these business ideas was put together to help you to make a decision about the best business for you and your family.

Many of the business ideas that are listed below will also require computer software. **Download.com (www.download.com)** provides free, try-for-free, or software-for-purchase that you can download right to your computer.

Now let's get started with the businesses you can start.

Affiliate Manager: ★ ★ ★

The affiliate manager maintains the entire scope of affiliate programs by assisting the business owner in creating the affiliate program or maintaining an existing one. Affiliate programs are offered through a variety of Web pages and businesses. For example, Atlantic Publishing Company has an affiliate program. If you log onto the company's Web site at **http://www.atlantic-pub. com/affiliate.htm** you can sign up or find out more.

Business Overview:

The affiliate manager focuses on maximizing an affiliate program, earning potential through creating and/or building the program from the bottom up, or restructuring an existing program.

Duties include:

- Motivation of affiliates to sell more products and keeping the affiliate up-to-date on new products and services offered by the client.

- Provide promotional material to the affiliate for the program.

- Recruit more affiliates for the program.

- Keep track of all sales by affiliates and write the commission checks.

- Train affiliates in the product and services of the client.

Show Me the Money: $$

The affiliate manager can offer their services on a monthly or per-project basis.

Business Equipment: 📞 📄 🕪 🖥 💿

You will need database software to keep track of affiliates, potential affiliates, and the earnings of each affiliate.

Business Base: 🏠 🌐

This is an at-home business with no travel time required.

Clientele:

Big and small businesses use affiliate programs to give incentives to Web sites for their advertisement.

Starting Point:

The starting point is when you first start seeking out a smaller business and asking if you can conduct the management of their affiliates to showcase your ability and to receive a letter of reference or recommendation.

Learn More:

Online

The Home Business Journal (**www.homebizjour.com**) offers articles, tips, news, and information for affiliate programs on the net.

Affiliate Programs (**www.affiliateprograms.com**) offers a variety of opportunities for the affiliate. This is a good place to find potential customers. Search through the affiliate opportunities to see what company has affiliate programs being offered.

Simply the Best (**www.simplythebest.net/affiliate_programs/**) offers information on affiliate programs and examines the best ones out there today. The Web is set up for you to search through a variety of programs on the market today in a number of different industries. This could be a great place to find prospective clients.

Books

The Ultimate Guide to Search Engine Marketing: Pay Per Click Advertising Secrets Revealed by Bruce C. Brown, (**www.atlantic-pub. com**, Item # UGS-01).

Astrologist: ★ ★ ★

Astrology is the art of interpreting, through math and related findings, the relative positions and movements of celestial bodies and the construction of celestial patterns to understand and organize information about personality, human affairs, and other terrestrial matters.

Business Overview: *

Interpret and organize the various patterns in an individual's chart to determine the course of their day, week, or year. If you enjoy mathematical equations, the mystery of the celestial bodies, and how they relate to each individual's birth, being an astrologist is the perfect position for you.

Your basic duties will include:

- Read charts

- Write your findings

- Analyze the charts with an individual's birth coordinates

You can also have your astrology reports become syndicated and be a syndicated columnist. See Syndicated Columnist this chapter.

Education/Skills:

Although no education is required for this job, you do need to understand the charts and how to read them. It would be a good idea to be certified in this field, though.

Show Me the Money: $$$$

Depending on your experience you can charge around $200 per chart.

Business Equipment: 📱 ☎ 📄 💿 🖥 ☽

You may need astrology software to help read, organize, and produce an individual chart. Some astrologists use them, while others do not.

Business Base: 🏠 🌐

This is an at-home position, unless you plan on giving seminars and party readings, which would only require about 40 percent travel time. Party readings can be a great way to make some extra money when starting out. With 10 to 30 guests, charging $20 per person, giving each person 15-20 minutes...think about the outcome.

Clientele: 💬

The vast majority of people who are interested in astrology can be found online or through various alternative healing seminars and groups. Businesses and investment companies are active in using astrology for current and/or future market stability.

Starting Point: 🔒

If you understand the core concept of putting a chart together, you can start by contacting newspapers, magazines, or local publications to offer your services in their paper on a monthly, weekly, or daily basis. You can review publications in every state by logging onto **www.newslink.org**. It might take some time to find a publication that does not already have an astrologist, but if you keep your search up, you are bound to find one.

You can also contact some small investors and ask if you can do a short financial review of the market to get started. When you have a lead and your chart is accurate you will have a professional referral. Because only certain amounts of people believe in astrology your clientele will be selective at first, until you become well known.

Learn More:

Online

Astrology Database (**http://www.astrologydatabase.com**) is a Web portal committed to astrology and the astrologist. With articles, books, Web links, and astrology software you will find everything you need to start using astrology as a tool for your own life or to provide astrological services.

The online College of Astrology (**http://www.astrocollege. com**) offers classes and information for those who are seeking to learn more about astrology or who wish to offer personalized astrology.

You can earn your degree in astrology through this prestigious UK astrology college (**http://www.astrology.org.uk/index.htm**).

Astrologist Susan Miller's Web portal (**www.astrologyzone. com**) has a vast amount of information about astrology and understanding astrology, and her in-depth monthly readers are found on this site.

Books

Identifying Planetary Triggers: Astrological Techniques for Predictions by Celeste Teal, Eila Savela.

Astrology 101: Beginner's Guide to Reading Your Chart by Gyan Surya.

Planets and Possibilities: Explore the World of the Zodiac beyond Just Your Sign by Susan Miller.

After School Program Director: ★ ★ ★

Do you have a knack for providing and developing programs for children? Do you have a skill you would like to teach children but do not have the venue? You can use an after school program to offer Bible classes, chess classes, singing lessons, acting classes, writing classes, or even investing classes.

Business Overview:

An after school program director not only creates and develops a class for elementary, junior high, or high school students, they also teach the class.

Your basic duties will include:

- Design the class

- Prepare the class work and the homework

- Schedule the class activities

- Provide details of the class and updates to the school system

- Keep in contact with parents and update them throughout the duration

Education/Skills:

There is no degree needed for this, but a teaching certificate can only help your chances of teaching students. No education is required to receive a teaching certificate; it costs around $15 to $20 depending on your city and state.

Show Me the Money: $$$

Depending on your experience you can charge around $200 per student, per class. Sometimes you can get a personal grant of $50,000 yearly to provide after school programs.

The Wallace Foundation (**http://www.wallacefoundation.org/WF/ GrantsPrograms/FocusAreasPrograms/Out-Of-SchoolLearning**) is one of many foundations that provides grants for after school programs.

You can search for grants on the U.S. Department of Education's home page (**http://www.ed.gov/index.jhtml**). You also can find a number of grant opportunities on various other sites like Grants. Gov (**http://www.grants.gov**).

These are merely starting points for your search. Be sure to get information on the grants you need. If you do not find the grant you are looking for online, stop by your local library, and in the business section you will find a large, red book, *Grant Select*, that has every grant offered in the world for everything from building your home to teaching after school programs. Ask for assistance from the librarian if needed.

Business Equipment: 🕾 📄 🖥 ☽

Depending on the type of class you are teaching your business equipment is minimal.

Business Base: 🏠 📠

This is an off-site position, although you will and should have a home office. The majority of your work is done at the school after the regular students have gone home. Therefore, the travel time is about 90 percent.

Clientele: 🗫

Your main clientele will be school boards in various school districts. Although you will be teaching students, the school will be your primary client.

Starting Point: 🔓

Develop your idea on paper and provide an outlined overview of the program you wish to implement. Contact your local school board and set up a meeting with one or all the members to offer your overview for the program that can be implemented in the following school year. Normally, the boards have funds set aside to fund after school programs. But they may have something similar in development; if so you can always go to the next school system.

If their budget is too low but they like your program idea, you can seek outside grants and ask them for a letter of referral or grant recommendation to put into your grant-seeking package.

Learn More:

Online

Middle Web (**http://www.middleweb.com/afterschool.html**) explores after school programs for the middle school student. It offers information on starting, maintaining, and getting funding for an after school program.

On the Department of Education's Web site (**http://www.ed.gov/index.jhtml**) you can find information on developing and maintaining an after school program.

An after school program resource for directors and after school program coordinators is **www.schoolagenotes.com**.

Books

Making Play Work: The Promise of After-School Programs for Low-Income Children by Robert Halpern.

A Place to Call Home: After-School Programs for Urban Youth by Barton Jay Hirsh, Nancy L. Deutch.

The Fifth Dimension: An After-School Program Built on Diversity by Michael Cole (Editor), Michael Cole.

Accounting Services: ★ ★

Do you love to crunch numbers? Do you provide accounting services for yourself or family and friends? If so, providing accounting services could be a very profitable business for you. Everyone needs an accountant whether for business or personal reasons; therefore, your potential clientele list is endless with online accounting services.

Business Overview: *

An accounting service provides the client with all relevant calculations for the IRS, state, and local taxes.

Your basic duties will include:

- Calculating finances.

- Preparing tax forms.

- Providing a detailed summary of tax information.

* For an additional income you can also provide bookkeeping services. See Bookkeeping in this chapter.

Education/Skills:

A degree in this area is very helpful, but not necessary to start an at-home service if you already know accounting. A CPA would greatly increase your odds of being hired.

Show Me the Money: $$$

Depending on your experience you can charge between $30 and $40 an hour.

Business Equipment:

In addition to the basic at-home business equipment you should also have accounting software, reference material, and a top of the line calculator.

Business Base:

This is an at-home business, although some travel may be required to meet with clients in their home or office. If you can receive faxes and documents through the mail, you can also offer your services online.

Clientele:

Your main clientele will be small business owners and individuals; after you have spent some time in the industry you can begin offering your services to larger businesses and corporations.

Starting Point:

Offer your services to churches or other nonprofit organizations for a tax break; this will gain you clientele, letters of referral, and a start in the industry.

Learn More:

Online

U.S. financial accounting and reporting standards (**www.fasb.org**).

A comprehensive index of tax and accounting resources on the Internet (**www.taxsites.com**).

National professional association for CPAs in the United States (**www.aicpa.org**).

Books

Accounting for Dummies and *Accounting Workbook for Dummies* by John A. Tracy.

Small Business Accounting Simplified by Daniel Sitarz.

Administrative Assistant: ✯ ✯ ✯

An administrative assistant offers a number of services to companies or CEOs in need of office help. An administrative assistant's duties can range from running errands to answering calls, going through mail, answering mail, or a variety of other administrative work.

Business Overview:

Administrative assistants are basically office hands that help with daily office duties. You can either offer your services in this manner or advertise as an office setup person, in which case you set up the file cabinets and get the office ready for its startup.

Basic responsibilities include:

- Filing
- Answering phones, e-mail, or regular mail
- Writing letters, faxes, or correspondence
- Typing
- Sending letters, faxes, or other correspondence
- Running errands
- Delivering papers or other important items
- Other office duties

Education/Skills:

No education is needed, but understanding office technicalities such as filing, answering phones, typing, and other office procedures will be helpful in providing these services.

Show Me the Money: $$$

The project length and how many other jobs you can obtain in a given year will greatly influence your annual earnings. You can charge per project, per time frame, or per hour.

Business Equipment:

No other equipment is needed, next to the basic home office equipment.

Business Base:

Much of the work can be done in a home office, but many CEOs may need your skills in their offices. This could turn out to be 30 percent in-home, 20 percent travel, and 50 percent out of home office.

Clientele:

Your clientele would be business owners locally or online. Sometimes at-home businesses could use your services to help them set up a home office.

Starting Point:

This job is fairly easy to break into. Start by searching through administrative jobs online and put up a Web site advertising your services. For local clients put an ad in the classified section of your newspaper.

Learn More:

Online

Resources and references for the administrative assistant or virtual assistant are available at **www.adminprof.com.**

Free tips, tricks, software, and other resources for administrative assistants are available at **www.adminassist.ca/tips.html**.

Information, resources, and employment opportunities for administrative professionals can be found at **www.adminassist.ca**.

Books

The Administrative Assistant by Brenda Bailey Hughes.

Administrative and Executive Assistant Career Starter by Shirley Tarbell, and Lauren B. Starkey.

Business Consultant: ☆ ☆ ☆ ☆

When a business gets into a tight spot with management, loss of sales, or their career goals are not being met they turn to a business consultant to help them get back on track. A business consultant comes in and reviews the company's problem and initiates an innovative solution to the problem.

Business Overview:

The business consultant works as a liaison between the president, the clients, and the employees.

Other responsibilities include:

- Enhance the company image

- Reformat sales and marketing plans

- Consult with current and former clients

- Improve promotional materials and products

- Evaluate the business plan and future goals

- Improving other aspects of the business, as outlined in the contract between you and the company president

A contract should be implicated before any work is done. The contract should outline the way you are paid (either by the project, by the hour, or by the week), and every duty you need to fulfill for your obligation to be satisfactory. Also have the owner/ president set his goals for the duration of time you will be with the company; for example, everything he would like accomplished in the business.

Education/Skills:

It would be beneficial to have a business degree or have a background in business management or consulting. You should understand the logistics of running a business and the proper formats to use when a business is failing.

Show Me the Money: $$$$

This is easily a six-figure income, after you have been established in the industry. Usually the annual pay averages $60,000 to $100,000.

Business Equipment:

There is no extra equipment with this business; of course you will need the basic office equipment as we discussed earlier in the chapter.

Business Base:

This is usually a 40 percent home business and a 60 percent in office business; you will need to spend a lot of time with the client to have an accurate view of what his career goals are for the business.

Clientele:

Mainly small- to mid-size businesses; you can also work with nonprofits, but you may have to adjust your rate to give them something they can afford. Another way to reach clientele is to offer startup business consulting. That way, instead of getting the company out of a hole, you can start them out on the right footing and steer them in the right direction.

Starting Point:

It would be a good idea to keep your current job or source of income while you are starting your consulting firm and as you begin to gain clientele. You should start with a Web site and advertise in your local paper or on small business and startup Web sites. If you are interested in giving a startup consulting for a referral or a very low fee, you can contact your local SCORE office and see if there is a startup company that would be in need of a free (or very low fee) startup consultant. If you do well, SCORE may keep your name handy for future reference and offer you leads to other companies that might need your assistance.

Learn More:

Books

Start Your Own Business Support Service (Entrepreneur Magazine's Start Up) by Entrepreneur Press.

Business Consulting: A Guide to How It Works and How to Make It Work (Economist Series) by Gilbert Toppin, Fiona Czerniawska.

Getting Started in Consulting, Second Edition by Alan Weiss.

Bookkeeping ☆ ☆ ☆

If you enjoy keeping records of daily activities and having the freedom of an at-home business with the benefits of a payroll employee, bookkeeping is the perfect job for you.

Business Overview:

Your basic duties will be to keep records of the business's earnings, losses, and payables. Other duties might include:

- Payroll
- Tax preparation
- Financial statements
- Billing
- Bank transactions

Education/Skills:

There is no room for errors or mistakes when you are keeping books for a company. It is important to have strict attention to detail when working in the bookkeeping industry. Bookkeeping is easier to get into than regular accounting services, and most employers do not ask for a CPA or any other accounting degree. Knowledge of basic accounting will be helpful in this field. You should also have a basic understanding of spreadsheets and accounting software.

Show Me the Money: $$$$

When you first start out you should offer your services for

somewhere in the $15 an hour range, but this can easily move up to $35 an hour after you gain some experience and have a handful of positive referrals.

Business Equipment:

You should invest in good accounting software and also have a variety of ledgers on hand. When you keep books you want to be sure to log the information in the computer and in the ledger, to have both available to the client.

Business Base:

Depending on your client's needs, this should be close to a 50-50 business, 50 percent at home while the other 50 percent is spent at the client's office.

Clientele:

This is strictly for the small- to medium-sized business; larger firms have human resource and other departments to keep the financial bookkeeping in line.

Starting Point:

Contact small businesses in your area to see if they are in need of a bookkeeper, place ads in the local paper, and become involved in your local chamber of commerce.

Learn More:

Online

Training to help you start and operate your own home-based accounting and bookkeeping business can be found at **www. accountbiz.com**.

You can start your own bookkeeping business with little more than a table for your computer and some good training. See **www.accounting-and-bookkeeping-tips.com.**

Resources for the bookkeeper are available at **www.allbookkeepingresource.com/homebizstart.htm.**

Bookkeeping tips and tricks can be found at **www.accountingandbookkeepingtips.com.**

Books

Bookkeeping for Dummies by Lita Epstein.

Step-by-Step Bookkeeping: The Complete Handbook for the Small Business (Revised) by Robert C. Ragan.

Start and Run a Bookkeeping Business by Angie Mohr.

Business Plan Writer: ☆ ☆ ☆ ☆

Do you enjoy writing and seeing the excitement of hopeful entrepreneurs? Then perhaps a career in business plan writing would be a perfect at-home business for you.

Business Overview:

Just as we have discussed in the previous chapter a business plan is the most important part of an entrepreneur's startup. It is the stepping stone to the future goals and success of the company; it is an in-depth look at every aspect of the business startup from financing for the following two to five years to what the goals of the business are and who the major players are. It is the entire backbone of a company, and some say it can make or break the company.

Your duties will include:

- In-depth research

- Provide sales and income projections

- Write the business plan

- Provide suggestive objectives and goals

Be prepared to spend at least a week researching and writing a single business plan; more in-depth plans may take longer. But the price for the plan will effectively make up for the time spent on the business plan.

Education/Skills:

Business development background would be extremely helpful, along with the understanding of financial and accounting procedures. You must be able to write clearly and effectively and provide thoroughly researched markets, competition analysis, and comprehensive goals, objectives, and future financial predictions.

Show Me the Money: $$$$

The normal charge for business plans are anywhere from $2,000 to $5,000, depending on the depth and length of the business plan. Being so, this industry can turn into a very lucrative business. With your annual income starting out at around $20,000 and, depending on your locale and clients, you can make upward of $100,000.

Business Equipment: 📱 ☎ 📄 🖥 💿 ◐

You should invest in business plan software, to be used in conjunction with the basic home office equipment we discussed at the beginning of this chapter.

Business Base:

This is an at-home business with 10 to 20 percent travel time or client office visits.

Clientele: ✒

Emerging entrepreneurs or small businesses looking for financing to expand their current business will be your main clientele.

Starting Point: 🔓

Put together a Web site, which emphasizes your services, along with a sample business plan that you wrote for a fictitious company that potential clients can read to review your ability. Advertise on small business Web sites. If you do not have the money to advertise, ask the site owner if you can trade links, where you point your clients to her and she points her clients to you; of course the owner would have to have a small business resource Web site, versus one offering business writing services.

Learn More:

Software

Business Plan Writer Deluxe at **http://www.novadevelopment. com/Products/us/brw/default.aspx**.

Online

An open directory project with links to hundreds of writing resources on the Web is **http://dmoz.org/Arts/Writers_Resources**.

Business plan writing 101 is available at **http://www. partnersinpublishing.ca/business_plan.htm**.

Books

Business Plans Kit For Dummies (For Dummies Business & Personal Finance) by Steven D. Peterson, PhD, Peter E. Jaret and Barbara Findlay Schenck.

The Complete Book of Business Plans: Simple Steps to Writing a Powerful Business Plan (Small Business Sourcebooks) by Joseph A. Covello and Brian J. Hazelgren.

Business Plans That Win $$$: Lessons from the MIT Enterprise Forum by Stanley R. Rich.

How to Write a Great Business Plan for Your Small Business in 60 Minutes or Less: With Companion CD-ROM by Sharon L. Fullen and Dianna Podmoroff.

Cake Decorator: ★

If you enjoy decorating cakes and you have a talent for making innovative and fun designs, it is time to turn that talent into some money.

Business Overview: *

Cake decorating can be a fun business. Your responsibility will be mostly baking.

There are two options that you can take with this business:

Option One: You can provide your services strictly out of your home, baking specialty cakes for birthdays, graduations, anniversaries, and weddings.

Option Two: You can rent a storefront and sell customized wedding cakes, cookie cakes, and cupcakes. You can also expand into a specialized cake bakery and offer a variety of bakery items

* To add income to this business you can also become a personal chef. See Personal Chef in Chapter 4.

Education/Skills:

For this business to work you must have a steady hand, attention to detail, and a little creativity. Knowledge of baking and the basic concept of making a variety of designs using cake decorating bags and tips will be helpful, although these skills can be obtained by purchasing some books on the subject, taking a class at your local craft store, or visiting some online cake decorating Web sites.

Show Me the Money: $$

The amount of money you can make depends on the option you choose:

Option One: You can expect to make anywhere from $5,000 to $25,000 annually.

Option Two: If you choose to have a storefront, you can expect to make anywhere from $40,000 to $60,000 annually. When you are established in the community, you will see an increase in your annual income.

Of course you can start out with option one, and after you have established a name for yourself you can ease your way into option two.

Business Equipment:

You will need a commercial oven, cake pans in a variety of shapes and sizes, decorative utensils, some great recipes, the ingredients for those cakes, and sometimes, decorative figurines. You might also want to begin a collection of cake decorating books for creative ideas and a variety of designs and instructions on how to produce them. If you plan to deliver your cake, a mid-sized van would be a good investment.

Business Base: 🏠 🚐

If you are sticking with option one and you plan on this being a home-based business, your travel time should be merely 10 to 20 percent, if you plan to deliver.

Clientele: 🗨

This will more than likely be a community-based business.

Starting Point: 💣

First you should check with the Food and Drug Administration and/or your local health department to be sure you do not need a license or inspections to offer your services. More than likely they will need to approve your space for commercial baking.

When you are approved as a cake decorating business, start by offering your services to local charity events, benefit dinners, or other media related humanitarian efforts. You can also sponsor a bake-off in your area; have all the area bakeries get involved and ask local businesses to donate prizes, such as gift certificates or coupons for their business.

Learn More:

Online

At one of the busiest times of the year, cake decorators are often expected to turn out wonderful Christmas cakes. A few ideas to make the season festive can be found at **www.cake-decorating-tips.com.**

Organization that encourages and promotes the art of cake decorating can be seen at **http://www.ices.org.**

Books

Professional Cake Decorating by Toba M. Garrett, Christine Mathews (Illustrator), Steven Mark Needham (Photographer).

Sweet Celebrations: The Art of Decorating Beautiful Cakes by Sylvia J. Weinstock Kate Manchester, Michelle Hickey (Illustrator).

Craft Show Organizer ✮ ✮

There is more than one way to make money off your crafts. You can also host or become a craft show organizer. You will then have to solicit crafters to rent a booth at your craft show.

Business Overview: *

Craft show organizers puts together the entire craft show from start to finish, setup to cleanup. Make the craft show fun and include other activities that might make a family come out for the day.

Education/Skills:

You do not need to have any type of skill or degree for this, but understanding event planning would be extremely helpful. Creativity is a must, though; think of inventive, themed craft shows that you can have, like a "Down on the Farm" craft event where crafters who produce farm replicas of any kind, even barnyard mailboxes, are asked to get a booth. Then ask local farmers to bring their farm animals and have a farmers market.

Show Me the Money: $$

You will just break even for the first few years; after that you should make anywhere from $20,000 to $40,000. But if you are also a crafter and you have a table at the craft show, you will have to have someone run the table for you, which could add another $20,000 annually.

Business Equipment:

The only extra equipment you might need is a planner, van, and crafting equipment.

Business Base:

This business averages a 50-50 split between at home and travel or outside office.

Clientele:

Your clientele will first be the crafters, then people purchasing crafts.

Starting Point:

Contact local venders about space, cost, and scheduling to rent the facility for an event. You will have to advertise in local crafter's newsletters, hobby shops, and various other crafter groups. Once you have a good amount of participants, you can begin advertising for the craft show itself and contact those who might have an affiliation with your themed craft show.

Learn More:

Online

The open directory project has links to hundreds of craft resources on the net can be seen at **http://dmoz.org/Arts/Crafts**.

Searchable database of art festivals and craft shows can be found at **www.artandcraftshows.net**.

Craft show ideas to make your craft show experience more profitable are available at **www.craftassoc.com/craftsh.html**.

Books

Making a Living in Crafts: Everything You Need to Know to Build Your Business by Donald Clark.

Start Your Own Crafts Business: Your Step-by-step Guide to Success by Jacquelyn Lynn.

Craft Business Answer Book: Starting, Managing, and Marketing a Home-Based Art, Crafts, Design Business by Barbara Brabec.

Crafts and Craft Shows: How to Make Money by Philip Kadubec.

Cleaning Specialist: ☆ ☆ ☆

Cleaning businesses really do clean up on the income end. If conducted well, you can really sweep the competition under the rug.

A cleaning specialist does not just clean houses; they also clean apartments, office buildings, restaurants, and other commercial buildings. Most people do not realize that most large corporations hire cleaners to deep clean once a week and to sweep thoroughly nightly.

Business Overview:

Whether you will be cleaning family houses or commercial buildings your duties will include:

- Clean up of debris
- Disinfecting of toilet areas
- Mopping floors
- Thorough dusting
- Polishing
- Deodorizing
- Thorough vacuuming

For other jobs, such as the cleaning of windows and curtains, you can charge extra, but be sure to put that in writing. Draw up a contract that states what duties you will perform. If you choose to clean commercial buildings, especially restaurants, you should be aware of a few things up front: Restaurants need to be cleaned every day; therefore if you do not have any other hands to help, you will have to be there on a daily basis. And there are only two times in the day that you can go to clean: the first few hours before they open in the morning or right after they close in the evening and when every person is out of the restaurant.

Education/Skills:

The only skills you need are a very strong work ethic and dedication to your business.

Show Me the Money: $$$$

Depending on how many accounts you have, this can be a lucrative business and some have surpassed $100,000 in annual income.

Business Equipment:

You will need an industrial or commercial vacuum cleaner with extensions. It is nice, for a little extra income, to have a floor buffer but it is not necessary. Keep up to date with new and improved cleaning products and use commercial strength cleaning products, which you should be able to purchase through a janitorial supply store.

Business Base: 🏚️

This business is only about 10 to 20 percent at home, for filing paperwork and creating invoices.

Clientele: 💬

Restaurants, commercial buildings, including professional offices and suites, and residential homes may be interested in your services.

Starting Point: 🔑

Contact restaurant owners and office managers to see if they have an in house cleaning staff or if they sub-contract their work out. You can announce your new services to them through direct mail and offer them a free week to rate your cleaning service against the competition.

Learn More:

Online

Secrets to starting a successful cleaning business are at **www. thejanitorialstore.com.**

Resources for individuals considering starting their own house cleaning business are available at **www.housecleaningbiz101.com.**

Information and books that show you how to start a janitorial or home cleaning service, including the complete bidding process are at **www.janitorial-and-home-cleaning-business-systems.com.**

Books

Start Your Own Cleaning Service by Jacquelyn Lynn, Entrepreneur Press.

How to Start a Home-Based Housecleaning Business by Laura Jorstad, Melinda Morse.

Start and Run a Home Cleaning Business by Susan Bewsey.

Copy Writing/Editing ★ ★ ★ ★

Copywriters write copy for advertisement, marketing, and corporate purposes. This can also include writing tech manuals and guides for software, Web content, and other media sources.

If you are copy editing, your job consists of editing copy, with the rule of thumb being to stick to the five C's: clarity, correct grammar, concise writing, comprehensible reading, and consistency. The job basically entails editing copy.

Business Overview:

Depending on the project and scope of the project, copywriters may also offer creative ideas to the preparation and presentation of the various forms of media.

Education/Skills:

You should have excellent writing and grammar skills and have a basic understanding of how the publishing industry works, whether you are writing copy for newspapers, online media, or various other print publications.

Show Me the Money: $$$$

Copywriting may start out slow, but once you begin to build up your clientele you will soar with earnings of around $20 to $65 per hour. Many fellow copywriters make upward of $100,000 yearly.

Business Equipment:

There is no other equipment required besides the basic office equipment.

Business Base:

This is strictly an at-home business.

Clientele:

Small businesses, publishing houses, newspapers, and other media related sites, as well as Webmasters and Web owners, may seek your services.

Starting Point:

You can apply for membership and search through job listings on Web sites such as **www.guru.com**, **www.elance.com**, and **www.professionalmoonlighters.com**. These sights charge a membership fee and a per base fee, but the clientele you will build up and the work you can potentially get is well worth the fees.

You can also contact local small businesses to offer a free copy project in exchange for a letter of referral or recommendation. Never offer your services free; you should always get publicity or something else in exchange.

Learn More:

Online

The National Writer's Union at **www.nwu.org**.

Search for jobs in your area or around the world at **http://craigslist. org/about/cities.html**.

American Copy Editors Society at **http://www.copydesk.org**.

Advice on starting a copywriting business can be found at **www.internetbasedmoms.com/articles2/copywriting.htm**.

Starting and running a copywriting business, a definition, and detailed explanation of copywriting is available at **www.entinst. ca/SC-Copywriting.htm**.

Books

Elements of Copywriting: The Essential Guide to Creating Copy That Gets the Results You Want by Gary Blake, Robert W. Bly.

The Copywriter's Handbook: A Step-By-Step Guide to Writing Copy That Sells by Robert W. Bly.

Start and Run a Copywriting Business by Steve Slaunwhite.

2007 Writer's Market.

---

eBook Producer/Publisher: ★ ★ ★ ★

Write and design eBooks for clients or write how to, philosophy, or informational eBooks. Just about everyone has something they could teach someone else or a few tricks to improve the current way of doing something. If you have something to share, let your expertise make it into the hands of the public.

You can also set up a Web site to produce and sell eBooks. You can solicit writers to submit the eBooks to your site, and you can offer the ones you think will be well appreciated by the public for a fee, and your clients can download them. You can offer the writers a percentage of the sales of their eBooks.

Business Overview:

Your list of duties for putting together an eBook site could get pretty hefty. Some of your duties will include:

- Soliciting writers to submit their eBooks

- Write eBooks

- Read each submission

- Decide which books are best to be promoted (only about four or five each month in the beginning, until you get a feel for a schedule)

- Edit the eBooks

- Promote the eBooks

    o Send out press releases

    o Submit the eBook to critics for industry reviews

    o Send out promotional advertisements

- Solicit for advertisement in the book

These are just the basic duties. Unless you get a partner to help you, these duties could wear you out in the first few months of business.

Education/Skills:

A publishing background or an English degree would be highly recommended. If neither of these applies to you, you should pick up a class or workshop about the writing and publishing industry.

Show Me the Money: $$

eBook publishing is a medium income industry; when your Web presence and popularity grows you can make more money from selling advertisements on your Web site and in the eBooks themselves. You will start out at about $20,000 to $40,000 annually; with advertisement sales that could easily jump to $80,000 annually.

Business Equipment:

eBook creator software, contracts for writers and illustrators, and, if you will be developing the Web site, Web design and development software, with e-commerce development will be needed.

Business Base:

This is merely an online company.

Clientele:

There should be no restriction on your clientele, depending on the genre and age group you choose to produce and target.

Starting Point:

Learn what you can about the publishing and eBook industry. Take some industry crash courses or workshops to get a better understanding of the industry mechanics.

Learn More:

Online

Articles and links to information and resources to selling eBooks online are available at **http://ezinearticles.com/?Selling-Ebooks?-Learn-How-to-Make-Your-Ebook-Sell&id=72896**.

Books

Ebook Publishing Success: How Anyone Can Write, Compile and Sell Ebooks on the Internet by Kingsley Oghojafor.

Millionaire's Guide to Ebook Publishing. Secrets of Ebook on Demand Publishing, Pay Per Click Advertising, and Web Marketing Revealed!

How to Write a "How-To" Book (Or Ebook) - Make Money Writing about Your Favorite Hobby, Interest or Activity by Shaun Fawcett.

From Entrepreneur to Infopreneur: Make Money with Books, E-books, and Information Products by Stephanie Chandler.

How to Write and Publish Your Own eBook in as Little as 7 Days by Jim Edwards, Joe Vitale.

Ebook Secrets Exposed: How to Make Massive Amounts of Money in Record Time with Your Own Ebook by Jim Edwards, David Garfinkel.

Aiming at Amazon: The NEW Business of Self Publishing, or How to Publish Books for Less, Sell Without Hassle, and Double Your Profit (or More) With Print on Demand and Book Marketing on Amazon.com by Aaron Shepard.

Event Planner: ✯ ✯ ✯

Do you enjoy the planning process? Does putting together events, parties, meetings, seminars, and other community events sound like pure joy to your ears? Event planning may be for you.

Business Overview:

Event planners put together major events by:

- Providing themed ideas
- Developing a timeline
- Finding and renting a hall or banquet facility
- Organizing a schedule for the event

- Purchasing the event supplies (rent tables, table linens, decorations, and so on)

- Hiring staffing for the event (caterer, DJ, or other professionals in the area)

- Purchasing and sending invitations

- Any other special requests made by the client

Event planners should treat everything like it is their own planned event. These events are important for your clients so make it memorable for them.

Education/Skills:

No education required, but impeccable attention to detail and good time management skills are essential for success.

Show Me the Money: $$$

Event planners normally charge around $25 to $50 an hour, or 10 to 15 percent of the total event cost, and can make anywhere from $40,000 to $150,000 yearly, depending on the amount of work you can take on.

Business Equipment: 📱 ☎ 📄 🖥 💿 ☾

Event planning software will help you stay organized and on top of all your contacts.

Business Base: 🏘 🏠

This will be about a 40-60 split of time; you will spend 40 percent of your time at home and the other 60 percent will be travel time.

Clientele: 🗣

Many large businesses and non-profits put on major events throughout the year.

Starting Point: 🔓

You can start by announcing your new business to local businesses and non profits by sending a formal letter or postcard announcement. You can also visit area vendors, party stores, banquet halls, and DJs to see if they are affiliated with any event planners; if not, let them know what you are doing and that you would like to offer them an affiliate link — which means you send entertainment business to them and they send potential clients to you. This is a great way to get your name out there and have an affiliation.

You can get an affiliation with:

- Banquet halls
- Photographers
- Party stores
- Caterers
- Rental stores
- Craft stores
- DJs or other forms of entertainment

You can also put an ad in the classified section of your local paper or provide party planning for small events for neighbors, friends, or family members as a way to get word of mouth advertising and gain referrals. Set up a Web site from your city directory online or have a personal Web site to showcase referrals, contact information, and/or photos of events you have put together.

Learn More:

Online

The International Special Events Society at **www.ises.com**.

Resources and information for the event planner are available at **www.eventplanningcenter.com**.

Event planning for business or pleasure at **www.thegreatevent. com.**

The ultimate resource for all of your party, wedding, and event planning needs can be seen at **www.partypop.com.**

Event planning, party, and wedding planner resources are available at **www.alltimefavorites.com.**

Wedding planning and event planning site links the consumer or wedding planner with the photographer, DJ, caterer, and so forth. Visit the site at **www.eventlinker.com.**

Books

How to Start a Home-Based Event Planning Business by Jill Moran.

Event Planning: The Ultimate Guide to Successful Meetings, Corporate Events, Fundraising Galas, Conferences, Conventions, Incentives and Other Special Events by Judy Allen.

Opportunities in Event Planning Careers (VGM Opportunities Series) by Blythe Camenson, VGM Career Books.

The Complete Guide to Successful Event Planning With Companion CD-ROM by Shannon Kilkenny, available at **www.atlantic-pub. com**, Item # SEP-01.

Floral Designer: ☆

Do you like arranging flowers and floral patterns? Whether you are interested in arranging silk flower patterns or designing personal or city curbside flower beds, you can earn an income while you are doing something you enjoy.

Business Overview:

Design and arrange floral patterns for individuals or businesses.

Education/Skills:

There are no educational requirements associated with this business.

Show Me the Money: $

Floral designers can make anywhere from $20,000 to $50,000 annually. You can also have a small greenhouse to grow and create small potted plants and herbs to make extra money.

Business Equipment:

Flower crafting equipment and a variety of sizes of pottery and vases are needed. You might also want a small greenhouse if you plan to grow plants.

Business Base:

This is mainly an at-home business, with some travel time required.

Clientele:

There is no set clientele group for this particular business.

Starting Point:

If you live near farmers market stands, you can see if you can offer your plants and flowers through them on consignment, which means you keep the flowers at their stand, and if they sell it, they collect the money and keep a percentage for housing it there. Other small businesses may allow you to sell your prearranged flowers at their shop on consignment as well.

Learn More:

Online

Become a floral designer, visit **www.ehow.com/how_8116_become-floral-designer.html**.

Get paid to create floral designs, start your own flower business, or open a florist shop. See **www.homebusinesscenter.com/how_to_start/florist.html**.

Try your hand at floral design. See **www.your-dream-career.com/floral-designer.html**.

Books

Flower Style: The Art of Floral Design and Decoration by Kenneth Turner, John Miller (Photographer), Fritz Von Der Schulenburg (Photographer).

Fabjob Guide to Become a Florist: Discover How to Get Hired to Create Floral Designs or Start Your Own Flower Shop by Alisa Gordaneer.

Encyclopedia of Flower Design by Judith Blacklock.

Freelance Writer: ★ ★ ★ ★

Do you enjoy writing? If you enjoy writing informational articles, interview pieces, feature articles, or newsworthy content, freelance writing can be a fulfilling career for you.

Business Overview:

A freelance writer's process is like this:

- They think of the idea or piece to write.

- Research the idea and find focused information about it.

- They write the article.

- Research the market to send it to.

- Write a query letter.

- Submit the query letter to a list of potential editors.

- Wait for a reply.

- If the editor replies with interest then the writer submits the article.

And this process continues. Freelance writing is a very competitive market, and it can take years before a writer receives his first purchase. Many well known authors and writers, Stephen King for example, were rejected a number of times before they had their first piece published.

Education/Skills:

Excellent grammar skills are imperative; therefore, an English or creative writing degree would be helpful.

Show Me the Money: $$

Freelance writers can make anywhere from $0.10 a word to $2.00 a word depending on the market and the writer's experience. Many freelance writers make around $50,000 annually.

Business Equipment:

Nothing more than the basic office equipment is needed.

Business Base:

This is a strictly at-home business.

Clientele: 🗩

Newspapers, periodicals, magazines, Web sites, and other forms of media will buy written content.

Starting Point: 🔓

A good starting point would be to find a small local market. Your church's or school's monthly newsletter would be a great starting point; ask the editors if you can write a short informative essay.

Once you are published for the first time, keep that clip on file and continue to query your local newspaper or presses in your area; the more times you get your name in print the better. As you get published, keep all your published clips on file, and when you contact the magazines you would like to get into, send them your published clips. Published clips refers to a copy of the place in the periodical where your name appears, not the entire article. Most editors in major markets want to be sure they are working with an experienced writer.

Learn More:

Online

This service charges a small monthly or annual fee, but is very helpful in finding potential buyers for your writing, as it includes every editor, publisher, and all markets in the entire world that buy writing, their submission guidelines, and what they pay their writers (**www.writersmarket.com**).

Packed with information, writing contests, resources, and editorial contact information for the freelance writer and every other genre of writer: **www.writersdigest.com**.

Find freelance projects for writers, designers, copywriters, and other creative fields at **www.guru.com** or **www.elance.com**.

Books

Starting Your Career as a Freelance Writer by Moira Anderson Allen.

Writer's Market 2007 (Writer's Market) by Robert Lee Brewer.

The Freelance Writer's Bible: Your Guide to a Profitable Writing Career Within One Year by David Trottier.

Graphic Design: ☆ ☆ ☆ ☆

Graphic designers create digital designs for brochures, logos, Web-based graphics, and a variety of other images for animation and new media.

Business Overview:

You will design images and artwork for a variety of formats and periodicals and edit and arrange designs for the client's specific desires.

Education/Skills:

An art or design degree or background would immensely help the success of your business; communication, marketing, and customer relation skills would also be helpful.

Show Me the Money: $$

Graphic designers can charge hourly fees of $25 to $35, per project fees of $175 to $300, sometimes more depending on the scope of the project, with an annual income of $30,000 to $60,000.

Business Equipment:

You will need design software, such as Paint Shop Pro, Adobe Photoshop, or other image design programs, as well as the normal business equipment for a home office.

Business Base:

This is strictly an at-home business. Although many offices hire in-house graphic designers, most continue to use the services of a freelancer.

Clientele:

Your biggest clientele will be publishing houses, small and large businesses, and other firms that use graphic design and design services on a regular basis.

Starting Point:

Start with organizations with job boards and bidding sights to find a graphic design posting that you can bid on. If you have no experience with other firms, offer the customer a low price for the job in exchange for a letter of reference or referral. It will be a good offer if the quality of work is high. This will in turn lead to more work for you and a client who will most likely come back to you and send other clients to you.

Learn More:

Online

The American Institute of Graphic Designers — **www.aoga.org.**

Bid on jobs relating to graphic design at **www.elance.com**.

Find graphic design gigs at **www.guru.com**.

Graphic design careers and resources — **www.allgraphicdesign.com.**

Books

The Graphic Design Business Book by Tad Crawford.

Starting Your Career as a Freelance Illustrator or Graphic Designer by Michael Fleishman.

Artists & Graphic Designers Market 2007 (Artist's & Graphic Designer's Market) by Mary Cox (Editor), Michael Schweer (Editor).

Graphic Artists Guild Handbook: Pricing & Ethical Guidelines (Graphic Artists Guild Handbook of Pricing and Ethical Guidelines).

Genealogy Researcher: ☆ ☆ ☆ ☆

Do you enjoy learning about the past and discovering the various aspects of the mystery of the family tree? Do you love to organize information and offer clients a better view of who they are and where they came from?

Business Overview:

Genealogy researchers research the entire family tree all the way back until they cannot search anymore. The job can be a tough, grueling, and frustrating process, but the pay can be extremely high. Your job duties include:

- Research family histories or event history
- Organize the information
- Write the family history or event report
- Print and bind the information

You can also publish your findings with a publisher if the information is useful to the public spectrum or self publish and sell your findings online.

Education/Skills:

Research skills and customer service are a must in this business. You can attend classes at your local community college; many have a family history program as well. For better paying jobs you should be certified in genealogy research. Excellent time management and organizational skills are a must.

Show Me the Money: $$$$

Many researchers make more than $100,000 yearly. Depending on the clientele and the length of the job you can charge anywhere from $400 to $5,000 per job.

Business Equipment:

Genealogy software and a high-speed modem with cable or DSL for faster surfing are important.

Business Base:

This is strictly an at-home business.

Clientele:

There is no set clientele group for this industry.

Starting Point:

Advertise through genealogy and history buff Web sites.

Learn More:

Online

Accreditation of Professional Genealogists at **www.icapgen.org**.

Board for Certification of Genealogists at **http://bcgcertification.org**.

See resources and tools at **www.ancestralbranches.com/tools.html**.

Find out how to become a professional genealogist at **www. genealogy.com/genealogy/20_hnkly.htm.**

Books

Researcher's Guide to American Genealogy by Val D. Greenwood.

Complete Idiot's Guide to Genealogy by Christine Rose, Kay Germain Ingalls, Kay Germain Ingalls.

Professional Genealogy: A Manual for Researchers, Writers, Editors, Lecturers, and Librarians by Elizabeth Shown Mills (Editor).

Gift Basket Designer: ☆ ☆ ☆ ☆

Personalized gifts are a big business. When you specialize in personalized gifts or niche markets you can get in on that business.

Business Overview:

Create personalized gift baskets that are specially ordered or are prearranged through a niche market. For example: Let us say your customer wants a gift basket for a gardener. Your basket would contain gifts that are specific to the gardener. You may have a pair of garden gloves, seeds for flowers or fruits and vegetables, a farmer's almanac, and other gardening equipment. The amount your customer wants to spend greatly influences the items you have in the basket and how many items would be included.

Education/Skills:

A flair for creativity and design, and a knack for fun, personalized, and specific items would be helpful.

Show Me the Money: $$$$

The size, cost of the gifts, and how many gifts are in the basket will influence how much you will charge per basket, but the smaller ones should be around $25 and can range up to $100. When you first start out it is estimated that you could make around $25,000, but depending on your primary market and the profit you make per basket you could make up to $200,000 annually.

Business Equipment:

You will need a variety of shapes and sizes of gift baskets. If you will be wrapping them, you will need a variety of colors of shrink wrap and a shrink wrap gun. Gifts can be purchased after the orders or you can have a handful of gifts already available to be placed in the baskets. You may also want large bows to put on the top of the basket and small cards or name tags.

Business Base:

This is strictly an at-home business, but there have been women who have expanded their business to a storefront after the business grew too big for their homes.

Clientele:

There is no set group for this business.

Starting Point:

You can start out by selling your gift baskets at craft shows or other art events. Make a handful of different baskets. If you are close to a holiday (mother's day, father's day, or other holiday), make a handful of baskets related to that holiday. You can also attend wedding shows and have thank you baskets with thank you gifts for the brides to give to their bridesmaids.

Another sales idea could be making NFL or sporting baskets for sports fans and selling them on consignment at NFL apparel shops. You will have to speak with the owner to see if he will allow you to sell them on consignment, which means he puts them on a shelf, and if they sell, you give him a percentage of the sale price.

Learn More:

Online

Gift basket instructions and ideas are available at **http://www.cajuncookingrecipes.com/gift_basket_instructions.htm.**

Lucrative resources for gift basket businesses on the go are available at **http://www.giftbasketbusinessworld.com/index.html.**

Books

How to Start a Home-Based Gift Basket Business, 4th (Home-Based Business Series) by Shirley George Frazier.

Marketing Your Gift Basket Business by Lonna Weidemann.

The Perfect Basket: How to Make a Fabulous Gift Basket for Any Occasion by Diane Phillips.

The Gift Basket Design Book: Everything You Need to Know to Create Beautiful, Professional-Looking Gift Baskets for All Occasions by Shirley George Frazier.

Grant Writer: ★ ★ ★ ★

Do you enjoy researching and writing specialized reports for nonprofits and small businesses? Do you enjoy working with nonprofit organizations and helping them obtain the funds to continue their humanitarian efforts?

Business Overview:

Grant writers research a variety of philanthropy organizations, private sectors, and governmentally funded grants that will help specific organizations continue their much needed community programs. Grant writers write a report on the nonprofit that is seeking to receive funding. A grant is almost like a business plan, as it offers the grant giving foundation a view of the nonprofit, what the nonprofit offers to the community, and how each dollar will be spent. Duties include:

- Finding the grant giving organization that will match the nonprofit's current needs (many times there are grants specific to programs for education, women's issues, children's advocacy, childhood abuse, and so forth).

- Download or request the guidelines for the grant you are applying for.

- Follow the specified guidelines for the grant request.

- Write the grant proposal.

- Create graphs, spreadsheets, and statistical data to back up the nonprofit's programs and community dedication.

- Write follow up letters or correspondence as needed to the grant giving company.

Education/Skills:

Good grammar, vocabulary, and writings skills are needed for you to be successful in this business. In addition, an understanding of grant giving and grant seeking procedures and the nonprofit sector would be helpful.

Show Me the Money: $$$$

Grant writers can make a tremendous amount of money if they are exceptional at their craft. They normally charge 5 to 10 percent of the grant money they are seeking, or they charge a per project fee between $500 for small projects and up to $5,000 for large projects. Annual earnings can top the $100,000 mark.

Business Equipment:

Other than basic home office equipment you will need a top of the line computer and DSL or cable Internet for faster searching.

Business Base:

This is strictly an at-home business.

Clientele:

Nonprofits and small businesses seeking grants will request your services.

Starting Point:

Offer your services to a nonprofit on contingency — you do not get paid. This will showcase your talent, and the nonprofit does not have to worry about paying you, especially if they do not have a budget. You can look for nonprofits to offer your services to online at **www.networkforgood.com** or **www.volunteermatch.com**.

Learn More:

Online

The Federal Register (**http://www.gpoaccess.gov/fr/index.html**) is the official daily publication for rules, proposed rules, and notices of federal agencies and organizations, as well as executive orders and other presidential documents.

Philanthropy News Digest is available at **http://foundationcenter. org/pnd/21century.**

The catalogue of federal domestic assistance can be seen at **http://12.46.245.173/cfda/cfda.html.**

List of U.S. governmental grants and information for obtaining small business loans and grants can be found at **http://usgovinfo. about.com/library/weekly/blgrantsources.htm.**

Books

Grant Writing for Dummies by Beverly A. Browning.

The Only Grant-Writing Book You'll Ever Need: Top Grant Writers and Grant Givers Share Their Secrets by Ellen Karsh, Arlen Sue Fox.

Webster's New World Grant Writing Handbook by Sara D. Wason.

I'll Grant You That: A Step-by-Step Guide to Finding Funds, Designing Winning Projects, and Writing Powerful Grant Proposals by Jim Burke, Carol Ann Prater.

Hired Companion: ☆ ☆

Do you enjoy working with people one-on-one? Helping them get through their day and making sure they are fed, healthy, and taking necessary medications? If you would like to do some good while you are making money, this is the perfect business opportunity for you.

Business Overview:

Whether you are being hired for a day, a week, or constant supervision a hired companion makes daily trips and runs errands for senior citizens or handicapped adults who live on their own, in nursing homes, or supervised group homes. The job entails:

- Daily check ins or phone calls

- Errands or driving the individual to the grocery store, doctor, dentist, or other appointments

- Scheduling appointments, if needed

- Making sure breakfast, lunch, and dinner are accessible for the individual

You may have other responsibilities depending on each individual's needs, but you should be aware that, if you are not a registered nurse, you are not permitted to provide nursing care responsibilities to the patient.

Education/Skills:

There is no required education needed for this opportunity, but a real care and concern for others would be a needed commodity.

Show Me the Money: $$

Your pricing will depend on your responsibilities and the personal care you provide. You can charge hourly or daily fees. Many hired companions make $20,000 to $40,000 annually.

Business Equipment:

A dependable vehicle is a necessity.

Business Base:

This is a purely traveling business; you might spend 10 percent of your time in a home office making needed phone calls and appointments.

Clientele: 🗨

There is no set group for this opportunity.

Starting Point: 🔒

You could contact nursing homes, hospitals, group homes, or other care facilities in your area to offer your services to individuals in current need of a companion. If the facility enjoyed your services, you could ask them to offer you a letter of referral or give your name to clients who might benefit from what you are offering.

Learn More:

Online

Employment opportunities and resources for the hired companion can be found at **www.companioncareofwa.com/ employment.html.**

Advantages, resources, and other valuable information is available at **www.visitingangels.com.**

Books

Start Your Own Senior Services Business (Start Your Own) by Jacquelyn Lynn, Charlene Davis.

The Concierge Manual, Third Edition by Katharine C. Giovanni, Ron Giovanni.

Ultimate Service: The Complete Handbook to the World of the Concierge by Holly Stiel, Delta Collins.

The Complete Legal Guide to Senior Care (Legal Survival Guides) by Brette McWhorter Sember.

House Sitter: ★

When people go on vacation what happens to their home? Are their personal belongings safe? You can make sure everything stays in place by offering house sitting services.

Business Overview:

Stay in homes or check in regularly and watch the personal belongings of families or individuals on vacation. Duties could include:

- Mowing the lawn

- Retrieving the mail

- Keeping the home neat and tidy

The owners may ask that you take care of other responsibilities, which the two of you will decide on.

Education/Skills:

No educational skills are needed for this business opportunity.

Show Me the Money: $

House sitters can make $200 to $500 per project, depending on the length and time the family needs your services. Many house sitters can make up to $20,000 annually.

Business Equipment:

There is no business equipment for this position.

Business Base:

This is a traveling business. You will be at home only about 10 to 20 percent of the time.

Clientele: 🐾

Homeowners going on vacation or who will be away will seek your services.

Starting Point: 🔒

Talk to homeowners that you know and those in your area. Put up flyers in community centers offering your service.

Learn More:

Online

Sitter resources are available at **www.oursitter.com**.

House sitting related articles can be seen at **www.housecarers.com**.

Interior Designer: ★ ★ ★

Do you enjoy designing the inside of people's houses or office buildings? Can you look at a room and know exactly what would make that room come alive? Can you talk to people for just a few minutes and know what design patterns would match their personalities perfectly? Then you have found the business that would work perfect for you.

Business Overview:

As an interior designer your duties include:

- Create a design to the customer's specifications

- Design the room, which may include

  o Painting   o Hanging borders   o Plastering

  o Painting murals or other wall drawing

- Clean up of the room

- Installing ceilings

Depending on your client's request you may have other responsibilities.

Education/Skills:

A flair for creativity and an understanding of individual behaviors will help you identify and associate personalities with certain design aspects.

Show Me the Money: $$$

Interior designers can make anywhere from $40,000 to $70,000 annually, whether they are charging $40 to $50 hourly or by setting a per project fee.

Business Equipment:

Tape measure, a CAD system, design software, current design reference books, and room ideas are great additions to the necessary home office equipment.

Business Base:

This is a business in which most of your time will be spent at your client's location; a mere 20 to 30 percent of your time will be spent at your home office.

Clientele:

Contractors will be major clients, as well as individuals looking to build, needing restoration, or who are planning on redesigning their home.

Starting Point: 🔓

Get involved in house and home shows and get in contact with local builders in your area.

Learn More:

Online

Fluff that house and earn money using your creative design skills. Find information at **www.housefluffing.com**.

Information and resources on starting an interior design business are available at **www.mydesignhelper.com**.

A directory for the interior designer can be found at **www.interiordesignbusiness.net**.

Books

How to Start a Home-Based Interior Design Business, 4th Edition (Home-Based Business Series) by Nita B. Phillips, Suzanne DeWalt.

The Interior Design Business Handbook: A Complete Guide to Profitability by Mary V. Knackstedt.

Interior Design Visual Presentation: A Guide to Graphics, Models, and Presentation Techniques, 2nd Edition by Maureen Mitton.

Incorporation Specialist: ★ ★

Incorporating a business can be a time consuming process, due to the filing and in-depth paperwork it takes. Many business owners do not have the time or patience to complete these tasks so they look for an incorporation specialist to do it for them.

Business Overview:

File, write, and present incorporation packages with duties that include:

- Advising the company on which business entity will work best for their company

- Filling out the necessary paperwork

- Meeting with the client for signatures and finalization

- Advising the owner on board or director meetings, stock certificates, offering franchising, and various other incorporation issues

You will essentially be providing the startup of the business for the owners.

Education/Skills:

You will need knowledge of the incorporation process and procedures and business laws, as well as good written and oral communication skills.

Show Me the Money: $$

Incorporation specialists can charge anywhere between $175 to $300 per project or $30 to $50 by the hour, with the potential for $20,000 to $50,000 in annual earnings.

Business Equipment:

The basic home office equipment is necessary with a top-notch printer. Books on business law and incorporation procedures would be helpful as reference material.

Business Base:

This is an at-home business with 20 to 30 percent travel time and meeting with clients.

Clientele:

Emerging business owners and small businesses looking to incorporate their current business will seek your services.

Starting Point:

Advertise in business periodicals, start a Web-based newsletter offering advice on certain aspects of business, and produce a Web site where people can sign up for your newsletter. You should also advertise on Web sites that offer information on starting a business.

Learn More:

Online

Information and resources for starting a new business are available at **http://entrepreneurs.about.com.**

Incorporation laws and information about incorporating can be found at **http://smallbusiness.findlaw.com.**

Find business products and service providers at **http://www. business.com.**

Books

Business Structures, (American Casebook Series) by David G. Epstein, Richard D. Freer, Michael J. Roberts, George B. Shepherd.

Corporations and Other Business Organizations 2006: Statutes, Rules, Materials and Forms by Melvin Aron Eisenberg (Editor).

Incorporating Your Business for Dummies by The Company Corporation.

Instructor: ★ ★ ★

Do you have a special talent that you would like to teach others? Whether this is a learned talent, computer knowledge, or a specific talent such as painting, sculpturing, singing, and so forth you can teach others how to do it and get paid for it.

You can have a variety of specialties, including:

- Dance
- Yoga
- Fitness
- Fire-arms
- Computer programming
- Karate
- Writing
- Singing
- Music
- Diving
- Making Gift baskets and Scrapbooks

These are just a few of the specialties that can be taught and provide you with an income.

Business Overview:

Instruct others on how to provide a specific talent or skill. Your duties may include:

- Writing a course syllabus
- Writing a schedule of activities or steps of learning
- Instruct the class on how to achieve success with this talent

- Provide learning activities

You can instruct individuals on anything from how to get on the Internet to making glass products or how to incorporate your business, even applying make-up or painting. As long as you can call yourself an expert, you can teach a class on that subject.

Education/Skills:

Good communication, writing, and speaking skills are essential to the success of an instructor. A knowledge or understanding of how to teach a class would be helpful.

Show Me the Money: $

You can charge anywhere from $25 to $150 per person per class session—with a class session being six one-hour sessions. The number of classes you teach in a year will affect your annual income, which could be anywhere from $20,000 to $40,000.

Business Equipment: ☽ ☉

No extra equipment is necessary.

Business Base:

The majority of your time will be spent in the classroom with about 20 percent of your time being spent in your home office.

Clientele:

There is no set group for the business.

Starting Point:

Contact local universities, community colleges, or adult education institutions to offer a syllabus of your class and to see if they offer classes similar to yours. Many of these facilities will ask for 25 percent of your earnings for housing the class.

You can also contact your local library to see if you can offer your class in one of their rooms. One other way to offer classes is to teach them online, either through a live chat you have on your Web site or through an e-mail discussion group, like Yahoo groups.

Learn More:

Books

Instructor Excellence: Mastering the Delivery of Training (Jossey Bass Business and Management Series) by Bob Powers.

Lessons from the Cyberspace Classroom: The Realities of Online Teaching by Rena M. Palloff, Keith Pratt.

Art of Public Speaking by Stephen E. Lucas.

Jewelry Designer: ✭

Do you love jewelry? Do you enjoy creating jewelry designs for necklaces, rings, bracelets, and pendants?

Business Overview:

Design and create a variety of jewelry whether it is specialty, pre-ordered, or pre-made.

Education/Skills:

A talent for creativity and an understanding of a variety of gems, beads, and other items for creating jewelry is needed.

Show Me the Money: $$$$

The type of jewelry you create will significantly justify your earnings. If you are working with gold and diamonds, you will charge much more than you would for a beaded necklace. You can expect to make anywhere from $25,000 to $75,000 annually.

Business Equipment: 📱 ☎ 📄 🖥 ☾ 💿 ⬚

You will need a magnifying class, pliers, vices, a variety of jewelry clips and clamps, molds, and melting equipment.

Business Base: 🏠

This is strictly an at-home business, although a storefront would significantly boost your sales and offer clients a place to see all your beautiful jewelry designs.

Clientele: 💬

There is no set group for this business.

Starting Point: 🔓

If you do not have a store, you should offer your clients a Web site where they can review your current designs and jewelry. You should also attend jewelry, craft, and trade shows. Offer a monthly contest to the community, perhaps nurses or teachers or another specialty group of people, showing your appreciation for their services in the community. This may garner more media attention.

Learn More:

Online

Jewelry making resources and links can be found at **http://jewelrymaking.about.com.**

Instructions, forums, and links to information on jewelry making are at **http://www.jewelry-making.com.**

Find jewelry making kits and resources at **http://www.makingjewelryfun.com.**

Books

Jewelry Concepts and Technology by Oppi Untracht.

Art Marketing 101: A Handbook for the Fine Artist by Constance Smith.

Life Coach: ☆ ☆ ☆

Do you enjoy working with and coaching people one-on-one? This business involves helping people find their life's path or coaching them on the steps to take to make their life more fulfilling and successful. Having a gift with people, having a winning personality, and an interest in helping people would make you a perfect candidate for a job as a life coach.

There are other coaching specialties that you can concentrate in such as:

- Business
- Parenting
- Success
- Fear
- Creative
- Time management
- Stress

Business Overview:

You can conduct 30 minute to one-hour phone sessions, Internet chats, or in person meetings with your clients.

Education/Skills:

You should become certified in life coaching or go through life coaching training programs. People skills, a compassion for life, and the passion for the success of others will help you succeed.

Show Me the Money: $$$$

Life coaches can charge $50 to $75 per 30-minute session or $75 to

$200 per hour session. When you begin to build up your clientele and word of mouth advertising, you should make anywhere from $60,000 to more than $100,000 annually.

Business Equipment:

You should only need the basic home office equipment.

Business Base:

This is an at-home business, unless there is a need for a face-to-face meeting.

Clientele:

There is no set group of clientele for this business.

Starting Point:

Start by giving a free life coaching session to a victim of domestic violence or women living in shelters, perhaps single mothers who are attempting to get out of violent relationships. Allow the media to be a part of the progress of your charity coaching; this could be an ongoing thing until the person finally meets success and a positive life. This would also bring you media attention and free advertisement.

Learn More:

Online

The International Coaching Federation is available at **www.coachfederation.com**.

Learn more about the life coaching industry at **www.life-coaching-resource.com**.

Get certified in the field of life coaching: at **http://www.coachtrainingalliance.com/**.

Articles, training programs, and certification information about becoming a life coach are available at **www.becomeacoach.com.**

Coach for Life at **www.coachforlife.com.**

Books

The Life Coaching Handbook (Paperback) by Curly Martin.

Coaching Manual: The Definitive Guide to the Process, Principles & Skills of Personal Coaching by Julie Starr.

Coach Anyone About Anything: How to Help People Succeed in Business and Life by Germaine Porché, Jed Niederer.

SUCCESS STORY: DIAMOND IN THE ROUGH COACHING

Massachusetts-based life coach Eileen Prince Lou of Diamond in the Rough Coaching, **www.DiamondIn-TheRoughCoach.com**, says enjoying other people, wanting to help, and having empathy for others are the keys to success in the life coaching industry.

"You have to have communication skills, be outgoing, enjoy people, and you have to want to help others," she says. Eileen Prince Lou started her business in 2003.

"I used to be a human resource professional when a client of mine suggested that I start a life coaching business. She had gone through the training herself and thought that I would also be suited for it. Ironically, she decided against pursuing a career in coaching."

Working for herself she enjoys the freedom to schedule her time according to her and her clients, as opposed to working for a firm. "I love what I do and the independence," she says.

She acknowledges that for some who own their own business finding new clients and scheduling can be a problem. To overcome that she says, "Work through it with referrals and join a professional organization."

SUCCESS STORY: DIAMOND IN THE ROUGH COACHING

Her advice to anyone who is attempting to break into the life coaching business: "Get excellent training, as I did."

Her philosophy: Achieve a more creative, fulfilling life by following your own path. As your champion, I will show you the way.

To visit Eileen Prince Lou or to make use of her life coaching resources log onto: **www.DiamondInTheRoughCoach.com**.

Manicurist: ★

Love to give woman a beautiful new look on their hands? If you can stand the smell and have a good ventilation system at home, this might be the perfect job for you.

Business Overview:

File, clean, and polish the fingertips and nails of clients. Design acrylics, nail tips, nail extensions, or gel nails for customers and paint the finished nail. You could encourage and advertise nail extension parties; this could be a teenage party package in which each girl is charged $25 to $30 per nail set, with a minimum of 15 girls and a maximum of 30.

Education/Skills:

Most states require you to be certified as a nail technician, which requires testing.

Show Me the Money: $$

Many manicurists charge $25 to $40 for a manicure and $30 to $60 for a nail set, which means around $20,000 to $50,000 annually.

Business Equipment:

Manicurist equipment, nail tips, extension tools, adhesives, and a variety of nail polish colors will be needed. You also may want to invest in an airbrush kit for French manicures, which are extremely popular.

Business Base:

If you live in a residential area, you will not get the permit needed to provide this service at home, so you likely will need to have a traveling business where you take your kit to other people's homes.

Clientele:

Young girls and women will seek your services.

Starting Point:

Go through the required schooling, which takes only about six to nine months, and apply for the state testing kit. After you have passed your state testing kit you can advertise for nail parties and begin giving in-home manicures.

Learn More:

Online

This course (**www.creativenailplace.com/training.htm**) is for the complete beginner wishing to learn all the skills needed to become a true professional nail technician.

Breaking into and succeeding as a nail salon owner, becoming a nail salon owner, starting a nail salon, and getting paid to paint nails information can be found at **www.stylecareer.com/nail_salon.shtml**.

Find Creative Arts Schools at **http://www.creativeartschools.com/cosmetology-schools/career/become-a-manicurist.htm**.

Books

Milady's Standard Nail Technology by Milady.

State Exam Review for Nail Technology by Milady.

Milady's Standard: Nail Technology - Exam Review 4E by Milady.

Manicurist (Nail Specialty License) (Career Examination Series) by Jack Rudman.

Medical Billing Coordinator

CAUTION: This career has been known to have scammers associated with it. Do not send money to unknown companies.

Medical billing can be a challenging job and requires a balance of understanding the insurance process and good time management. But if you enjoy regular office work that you can do from home, this will be the perfect career for you.

The growing need for medical billing coordinators has created a scamming industry associated with this field. Never send an outside company money to start a job, receive a kit, or earn a degree in this industry.

Business Overview:

Your business duties will include:

- Invoicing

- Billing patients and Medicare

- Collecting co-pays

- Tracking past due accounts

- Answering patient's questions about billing

- Keeping the doctors informed

- Keeping up-to-date with insurance trends and medical billing changes

Education/Skills:

Knowledge of Medicare and Medicaid regulations, insurance billing, and Current Procedural Terminology (CPT) coding would greatly increase your chances of success. You can take a local class or seminar at your community college or adult learning center.

Show Me the Money: $$$

For this business to be profitable, you should have at least six accounts, which would be easy to handle and give you a potential annual income around $60,000 at a monthly rate of $800 per doctor.

Business Equipment:

You will need medical billing software, along with a very good printer and fax machine.

Business Base:

This is an at-home business, with maybe 5 to 10 percent of travel to your clients' offices.

Clientele:

Doctors, dentists, and other professional health care providers working in a private practice will seek your services.

Starting Point:

Design a Web site where visitors or medical health specialists can learn more about you and your services. Advertise on medical and professional health service Web sites. Send an announcement letter to health professionals in your area offering your new services with a free month or other specials to introduce your services.

Learn More:

Online

Medical billing association for professional medical billing and electronic claims processing can be seen at **www.ambanet.net**.

Find a billing business plan at **www.medicalbillingandcoding. net/billing_business_plan.htm**.

Start your own medical milling at-home business. Find info at **www.santiagosds.com/stepstosuccess.asp**.

Medical coding and billing books and software, with a trusted career guide and job resource for medical coding and billing students and professionals can be found at **www.medicalcodingandbilling. com/coding_bargains.htm**.

Medical billing software for the medical billing professional is available at **http://www.medicalbillingsoftware.com**.

Medical billing association for professional medical billing and electronic claims processing consultants is at **www.ambanet.net/ AMBA.htm**.

Books

Start Your Own Medical Claims Billing Service (Entrepreneurs Magazine Startup) by Entrepreneur Press.

Setting Up Your Medical Billing Business: Step-by-Step Procedures for

Starting and Managing a Computer-Based Electronic Medical Billing Business by Merlin B. Coslick.

Understanding Health Insurance: A Guide to Professional Billing by Jo Ann C. Rowell.

Mystery Shopping Specialist: ✮ ✮ ✮

CAUTION:	This career has been known to have scammers associated with it. Do not send money to unknown companies.

You have seen the scams advertised almost everywhere you look: Pay this amount of money and be a mystery shopper. You should not have to pay to become a mystery shopper. You can save yourself the trouble and instead of just being a mystery shopper, you can start your own mystery shopping business.

Business Overview:

Companies and restaurants hire mystery shoppers to rate the employee/shopper relationship, the store's cleanliness, and other issues the store has had complaints or concerns about. Many restaurants have a mystery shopper come in once a week.

Education/Skills:

There is no educational degree needed. Good communication skills and customer relations experience are helpful.

Show Me the Money: $$$

You can charge a per hour or per project fee. Because you are receiving gift certificates to buy products you might have to include the cost in your rates. If you own a mystery-shopping firm, you can make upwards of $60,000, depending on how many clients you have.

Business Equipment:

You might want to purchase a database software program to keep track of each shop you have rated, along with the ratings and comments for future use. You will also want to keep track of the businesses that have used your service in the past.

Business Base:

This business has only a 10 to 20 percent at home time period; the rest is travel time.

Clientele:

Any business that has customer relations, especially shopping facilities and restaurants, will seek your services.

Starting Point:

Contact businesses nationally who have chain stores in your area and announce your business, along with your business concept, which should be something like, "You shouldn't have to worry about what customers think—you should know." Let them know your prices and your methods for shopping/dining out (how you plan to rate the services). You can also put together a Web site and advertise online with various business and office product stores.

Learn More:

Online

A how to become a mystery shopper guide is available at **http://www.fabjob.com/mysteryshopper.asp**.

Customer Service Experts can be found at **http://www.customerserviceexperts.com/applyToShop.php**.

Online forum with information and the ability to meet certified secret shoppers can be found at **http://www.mysteryshop.org/shoppers/forum/**.

Books

How to Start and Run Your Own Mystery Shopping Company by Julie Weis, Lynette Janac.

Mystery Shopper's Manual, 6th Edition by Cathy Stucker.

How to Become a Mystery Shopper: The Only Book You'll Ever Need by Elaine Moran.

Public Relations Specialist: ✩ ✩ ✩

A public relations specialist is the primary door that leads the public to a company, service, nonprofit, or product. When a small company needs an advertising campaign, when something negative happens to a firm and they need a positive angle on it, when a campaign is in trouble, when a nonprofit needs its message to be spoon-fed to the public, who do these people turn to? A public relations specialist, and with so many companies cutting back on their in-house staff, a home-based public relations specialist is right there to pick up the pieces. Are you up for the challenge?

Business Overview:

A public relations specialist's job includes:

- Providing a positive image of the company they are working with to the public

- Keeping in contact with local media

- Creating media and public awareness campaigns

- Producing new mottos or logos for the company or their products or services

- Presenting creative new campaigns and colorful, catchy advertisements

Education/Skills:

An understanding of a variety of media and how they work, deadlines, current needs, likes and dislikes of each of those media branches will be helpful in this career.

Show Me the Money: $$$

You can charge a per project fee of $600 for small projects and up to $20,000 for larger projects or an hourly rate of $40 to $65, with an annual income somewhere in the $40,000 to $70,000 range.

Business Equipment:

You will need database software to keep track of media relations and clients, in addition to the basic office equipment.

Business Base:

Half of the time is spent at your home office and half is spent traveling or in the public.

Clientele:

Small businesses or large businesses that do not have in-house PR will seek your services.

Starting Point:

Contact a small business that is having a hard time or has had some bad publicity in the past and work on contingency. If things pick up with their business after your campaign, you get paid. This is also a great way to get the media involved in a community cares program—businesses offering their services to fellow business owners in trouble. You could actually start a Web site for that, as a sister site of your PR Web presence.

Learn More:

Online

Public Relations Society of America is at **www.prsa.org**.

Yvonne Buchanan explains how to start your own virtual public relations business at **www.homebiztools.com/ideas/public_relations.htm**.

A business plan for those looking to start a home public relations firm is available at **www.allbusiness.com/forms/board/479.html**.

Books

Public Relations for Dummies by Eric Yaverbaum, Ilise Benun.

How to Be Your Own Publicist: Everything You Need to Know to Act like a PR Pro by Jessica Hatchigan.

Public Relations: Managing Competition and Conflict by Glen T. Cameron, Dennis L. Wilcox, Bryan H. Reber.

Strategic Planning for Public Relations by Ronald Smith.

Pet Sitter: ✯ ✯

Do you love animals? Professional pet sitters are more than just a walk-your-dog-for-an-hour business. This is like babysitting, but with an animal. The profession has grown into the thousands, due largely in part to the number of households and families having family pets.

Business Overview:

Professional pet sitter duties include:

- Walking the animals on a regular basis

- Keeping them while the family is away

- Taking them to vet appointments

- Visit pets

There may be other responsibilities the owner could have you do, which is something that you must discuss with the client. To make extra money with this business you can also offer animal training sessions. See Animal Trainer this section.

Education/Skills:

A love for animals and knowledge of animal behavior and health are useful.

Show Me the Money: $$

Pet sitters can make anywhere from $20,000 to $40,000 annually, depending on how many pets they care for in a week. Average charge per pet is around $15 to $20, which can be charged per walk or per hour.

Business Equipment:

There is no other business equipment needed, unless you plan to have your own dog leashes and animal treats.

Business Base:

This is a traveling business. You may spend a mere 10 to 20 percent of your time in your office.

Clientele: 📢

Animal owners will seek your services.

Starting Point: 🔑

Contact local shelters to offer your services to animals without owners. Develop an animal walk-a-thon for animals in shelters; any proceeds for the event can go to local shelters. Contact the local media about the event, and ask your friends and family to get involved by taking an animal from the shelter for a walk. Contact veterinarians, pet stores, animal hospitals, pet groomers, and animal boarding houses to offer affiliate services with them.

Learn More:

Online

Pet Sitters International is at **http://www.petsit.com.**

A pet sitting directory and association for professional pet sitters can be found at **www.petsits.com.**

National Association of Professional Pet Sitters is at **http://www. petsitters.org.**

Wish Bones for professional pet sitters can be seen at **http://www. wishbonesforpets.com.**

Books

Start Your Own Pet Sitting Business (The Startup Series) by Cheryl Kimball.

Pet Sitting for Profit: A Complete Manual for Professional Success (Howell Reference Books) by Patti J. Moran.

Start Your Own Professional Pet-Sitting Service + FORMS (CD-ROM) by David A. Grass.

How to Start a Home-Based Pet Care Business, 2nd (Home-Based Business Series) by Kathy Salzberg.

Professional Researcher: ☆ ☆ ☆ ☆

Whether you are doing research for a doctor, editor, business owner, or publishing company, your work will be an integral part of theirs. Professional researchers provide all the necessary information to help other professionals do their jobs accurately.

Business Overview:

Research can be a grueling and time consuming job, but research is not all you will need to do. Other duties include:

- Read and research information from periodicals, online, and through various other published works

- Write a report and detailed list of the information you obtained

- Write a report from audio tracks of information provided from the client or other sources

Other duties may be involved that include detailing your findings in an audio version or other multimedia format.

Education/Skills:

Good oral communication and writing skills are a must, as well as an understanding of research, libraries, and how to obtain information.

Show Me the Money: $$$$

Professional researchers can make a lucrative living once they establish themselves in the industry. Some make well over the

$100,000 mark, charging $50 to $75 hourly or a per project fee of $200 to $1,000 or more.

Business Equipment:

Research software and database software, reference books, and other research information materials will be needed.

Business Base:

This is strictly an at-home business.

Clientele:

There is no set group for this business.

Starting Point:

Find research jobs on job boards such as **www.elance.com** and **www.guru.com**, as well as the other boards listed at the beginning of this chapter.

Learn More:

Online

Library of Congress Resources for Researchers are available at **http://www.loc.gov/rr.**

Association of Professional Researchers for Advancement is at **http://www.aprahome.org.**

Search engine for professional researchers can be found at **http://www.pro-researcher.co.uk.**

Books

Professional Genealogy: A Manual for Researchers, Writers, Editors, Lecturers, and Librarians by Elizabeth Shown Mills.

Rental Agent: ☆ ☆

Do you enjoy searching through rental properties, reviewing the far-off locations, and/or relating to those in your community? Have you ever thought that doing just that could make you a little extra money?

Business Overview:

A rental agent works just like a real estate agent, except you are not trying to sell a house. You are actually working for the renter and finding them a piece of renter's heaven.

You will search for rental properties in the price range and area indicated by your client, as well as room specifications. You might also meet with the owner of the property or the property manager. Whether this will be a place to call home for your client or a place to vacation, it will be your job to make the transition as easy as possible.

This would be a good opportunity if you live in an area where tourism is big business, as you can run a "Let me find your vacation home" Web site. You can take photos of the home for your client and upload those to your site, meet with the landlord, and take all the necessary steps for your client while he is miles away.

Education/Skills:

Knowledge of your area and good customer service skills would be a great business advantage.

Show Me the Money: $$

You can charge $25 to $40 hourly or on a per project basis, although this way you could spend six months looking for an apartment for a job that paid for two months. You can figure on making $25,000 to $40,000 annually.

Business Equipment:

If you live in a tourist hot spot, a digital camera would be needed, in addition to all the basic home business equipment.

Business Base:

This is 50 percent home-based and 50 percent road-based.

Clientele:

Renters will be your clients.

Starting Point:

Put up a Web site offering your services and advertise on rental Web sites and in local magazines that publish apartment rentals.

Learn More:

Most rental agents live abroad, but you can review how those in other countries conduct their business by contacting them.

Online

Holiday Rental Agents in Portugal are available at **http://www. portugal-info.net/holiday-rental-agents/index.htm.**

Rental Agents in San Miguel are available at **http://www.infosma. com/accommodations/rental-agents.htm.**

Syndicated Columnist: ✫ ✫ ✫ ✫

Are you the next Ann Landers? Do you have an advice column, gossip column, this date in history information, a humor column, or any other small offering like a puzzle or American fun facts? If you have something short and sweet and it could appeal to millions, you could be a syndicated columnist.

Business Overview:

Syndicated columnists write one short piece daily, weekly, bi-weekly, or monthly and submit that to his or her syndication or syndications, if you plan on being self-syndicated.

Education/Skills:

Writing skills and a quick wit are important to this business if you are writing a personal, advice, gossip, or other commentary column. Timeliness is also important, as each newspaper has a certain deadline you will need to meet.

Show Me the Money: $$

The number of markets (newspapers) your column runs in will influence your income, but if you are working with a syndicate, they will take a portion of your income. Syndicated columnists can make anywhere from $35 to $50 for their work. Multiply that by the number of newspapers that have picked it up, usually between 100 and 500. That averages out to be around $20,000 to $60,000 annually, but then you will give a cut to the syndicate. And that is only writing one short piece a week.

To eliminate giving a cut away you can always self-syndicate your column, meaning you send a submission to each newspaper you would like to be published in, which could be as many as a thousand and as little as a few hundred. You will still only write one column weekly, but you will have to send it to each editor that accepts weekly, bi-weekly, or monthly.

Business Equipment:

You will only need the basic at-home business equipment.

Business Base:

This is strictly an at-home business.

Clientele:

Newspaper editors and publishers of online ezines will be your primary clients.

Starting Point:

Put together a syndication package as the syndicate you would like to be published with describes. Some syndication will be different, so adhere to the guidelines accordingly. The online links are companies who you can submit your column to, but most ask for about 8 to 10 columns at first, so make sure they are the best you have.

For self-syndication you will need to contact editors yourself with a query letter and offer the column directly to them. This will eliminate the middle man (the syndicate) and bring you in direct contact with the editors. To find every newspaper worldwide with contact information log onto **www.newslink.org**.

Learn More:

Online

Read this article about getting your column accepted into a daily newspaper: **http://www.writersdigest.com/articles/ferle_ newspaper_column.asp.**

How to be a Syndicated Columnist eBook can be found at **http:// www.booklocker.com/books/545.html.**

The following online links offer submission policies to the top three syndicates:

King Feature submission guidelines — **http://www.kingfeatures. com/subg_column.htm.**

Comics Page submission guidelines — **http://www.comicspage. com/submissions.html.**

Creators submission guidelines — **http://www.creators.com/ submissions.html.**

Books

You Can Write a Column by Monica McCabe-Cardoza.

You Can Be a Columnist: Writing and Selling Your Way to Prestige by Charlotte Digregorio.

Syndication Secrets: What No One Will Tell You! by Jodie Lynn.

Syndicated Cartoonist: ☆ ☆ ☆ ☆

Are you the next Family Circle? Can you draw and write funny captions? Can you create panel cartoons that get a laugh?

Business Overview:

Provide pencil drawings with funny captions to editors and/or a syndicate.

Education/Skills:

You should understand cartoons and how they work and submitting to newspapers and syndicates. This can be easily learned through books and periodicals.

Show Me the Money: $$

The number of markets (newspapers) your cartoonist runs in will influence your income, but if you are working with a syndicate, they will take a portion of your income. Syndicated cartoonists can make anywhere from $35 to $50 for their work. Multiply that by the number of newspapers that have picked it up, usually between 100 and 500. That averages out to be around $20,000 to $60,000 annually, but then you will give a cut to the syndicate. And that is only drawing one short piece a week.

To eliminate giving a cut away you can always self-syndicate your cartoon, meaning you send a submission to each newspaper you would like to be published in, which could be as many as a thousand and as little as a few hundred. You will still only draw one cartoon weekly, but you will have to send it to each editor that accepts weekly, bi-weekly, or monthly.

Business Equipment:

An artist's table, drawing pencils, and drawing equipment are necessary, as well as the basic home office equipment.

Business Base:

This is strictly an at-home business.

Clientele:

Newspaper editors and publishers of online ezines will be your clients.

Starting Point:

Put together a syndication package as the syndicate you would like to be published with describes. Some syndication will be different, so adhere to the guidelines accordingly. The online links are companies who you can submit your cartoon to, but most ask for about eight to ten cartoons at first, so make sure they are the best you have.

For self-syndication you will need to contact editors yourself with a query letter and offer the cartoon directly to them. This will eliminate the middle man (the syndicate) and bring you in direct contact with the editors. To find every newspaper worldwide with contact information log onto **www.newslink.org**.

Learn More:

Online

The following online links offer submission policies to the top three syndicates:

King Feature submission guidelines — **http://www.kingfeatures. com/subg_comic.htm.**

Comics Page submission guidelines — **http://www.comicspage. com/submissions.html.**

Creators submission guidelines — **http://www.creators.com/ submissions.html.**

Books

Successful Syndication: A Guide for Writers and Cartoonists by Michael Sedge.

Cartoonists' and Illustrators' Trade Secrets by Robin Hall.

How to Draw and Sell Cartoons: All the Professional Techniques of Strip Cartoon, Caricature and Artwork Demonstrated by Ross Thompson, Bill Hewison.

Tutor: ★ ★

Do you enjoy working one on one with others, primarily children? Tutors can make a huge difference in a person's life.

Business Overview: *

Tutors work one-on-one with children and individuals in a range of areas. You can be a tutor that will help with all areas or you can be a specialty tutor of:

- Reading
- Math
- English
- Computers

- Science
- History
- Government
- College Prep

To add income to this profession you can add class time and be an instructor. See Instructor in this chapter.

Education/Skills:

"Patience is a virtue" is not just a saying with this line or work. You need to have patience of steel to work as a tutor. Although a teaching degree is not needed a degree in the area of the specific field of study would increase your odds of obtaining clients. Good communication skills are required to adequately educate the individual.

Show Me the Money: $$$

For personal instruction you can charge anywhere from $30 to $125 per hour or charge a per project fee (per project meaning until your client comprehends the material). Annually, tutors can make anywhere from $20,000 to $75,000.

Business Equipment:

You may need reference books.

Business Base: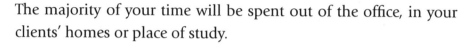

The majority of your time will be spent out of the office, in your clients' homes or place of study.

Clientele:

There is no set group for this business, but students, the newly employed, parents seeking help for their school-age children, and teens enrolling in college will make up the majority of your clientele.

Starting Point:

Contact schools and other vocational institutes to offer your services to children or adults in their organizations. Get involved with a professional organization

Learn More:

Online

The American Tutoring Association is available at **http://www.americantutoringassociation.org.**

Resources page can be found at **www.chalksite.com.**

Mayfair Tutors are at **www.mayfairtutors.pbwiki.com.**

Reading-Tutors resources can be seen at **www.reading-tutors.com.**

Books

Tutoring as a Successful Business - An Expert Tutor Shows You How by Eileen Kaplan Shapiro.

The Practical Tutor by Emily Meyer, Louise Z. Smith.

Technical Writer: ★ ★ ★ ★

Can you write on issues such as computers, computer science, medicine, communications, and other technical fields? Technical writing can be a lucrative business because of the amount of information needed for this field, the constant change and upgrade in technology, and the topic being difficult to explain. If you can write about it, you will have a steady income for years to come.

Business Overview:

Write and edit a variety of publications concerning the technical fields, including:

- Technical books
- Technical articles for trade magazines
- Publicity materials
- Instruction booklets for hardware and software
- Web site content, including SEO articles and ISO documents
- Policy and procedure manuals
- Brochures, flyers, and other desktop publishing materials
- Marketing pieces

Education/Skills:

Knowledge or a background in computers, computer science, medicine, communication, and scientific fields such as chemistry, engineering, and electronics are a necessity for this industry.

Show Me the Money: $$$

Charge a rate of $35 to $50 hourly or a per project fee of $300 to $1,200, depending on the amount of writing and time spent. Technical writers can make anywhere from $30,000 annually just starting out to $75,000 annually in the prime of their career.

Business Equipment:

The basic home office equipment, plus reference books and database software, will be needed.

Business Base:

This is strictly an at-home business.

Clientele:

Individuals, editors, and business owners in the technical fields will seek your services.

Starting Point:

Start with any number of the job boards provided at the beginning of this chapter to gain clients and jobs.

Learn More:

Online

Resources for technical writers are available at **www.writerswrite. com/technical/techlink.htm.**

Mailing lists, professional associations, feature stories, and news for technical writers at **www.techpubs.com/resources.html.**

Search for technical jobs online at **www.online-writing-jobs.com.**

Books

Technical Writer's Handbook: Writing With Style and Clarity by Matt Young.

Technical Writing 101: .'. Real-World Guide to Planning and Writing Technical Documentation, Second Edition by Alan S. Pringle, Sarah S. O'Keefe.

Developing Quality Technical Information: A Handbook for Writers and Editors (2nd Edition) (IBM Press Series--Information Management) by Gretchen Hargis, Michelle Carey, Ann Kilty Hernandez, Polly Hughes, Deirdre Longo, Shannon Rouiller, Elizabeth Wilde.

Transcriptionist: ☆ ☆ ☆ ☆

The medical transcription industry is a $50 billion industry. Are you ready to grab some of that income? There are two types of transcription you can get involved in: legal and medical.

Business Overview:

Transcription is the process of typing what is dictated in a tape recording.

- **Medical** — Type, dictate, and edit medical material from audio recordings and medical records.

- **Legal** — Type, dictate, and edit legal material from audio recordings and legal records.

Education/Skills:

Good grammar and communication skills are important.

- Medical — An understanding of the medical field and medical jargon.

- Legal — An understanding of the legal field and legal jargon.

Show Me the Money: $$$

You can charge $15 to $40 hourly, by the line, per project, or per typed page and make an annual income of $35,000 to $80,000.

Business Equipment:

Reference books, medical or legal software, and a transcribing unit will be helpful.

Business Base:

This is strictly an at-home business. You may have slight travel time to and from clients' office, which would only equal around 10 to 20 percent of your time.

Clientele:

Professional law firms, lawyers, medical offices, hospitals, doctors, and other professionals in your area or online will seek your services.

Starting Point:

Put together a business Web site for professionals to view your services and service prices.

Learn More:

Online

Resources for medical transcriptionists, the one-stop MT reference guide are at **www.transcriptionresource.com.**

Useful medical transcription sites, services, and resources for training can be found at **www.medilexicon.com/medicaltranscription.php.**

Resources for work at home transcriptionists are at **http:// mtresourcez.tripod.com.**

American Association for Medical Transcription at **http://www.aamt.org.**

Earn a degree in legal transcription at **www.uscareerinstitute.com/legaltranscription.asp.**

Resources for legal and medical transcriptionists can be seen at **www.transcriptionmatters.com.**

Books

Start Your Own Medical Claims & Transcription Business (Start Your Own Business) by Prentice Hall.

How to Become a Medical Transcriptionist by George Morton.

The Independent Medical Transcriptionist: The Comprehensive Guidebook for Career Success in a Medical Transcription Business by Donna Avila-Weil, Mary Glaccum.

Medical Transcriptionist Desk Reference by Carolyn Collins-Gates.

Medical Transcription Guide: Do's and Don'ts (Medical Transcription Guide) by Marcy O. Diehl.

Translator: ☆ ☆ ☆

Can you speak and write a different language fluently? Translators can work in both oral and written translation. Currently there are very few translators; therefore, this field is easy to break into and accessible.

Business Overview:

Translate your language specialty into English, or vice-versa, in both oral and written form.

Education/Skills:

A degree or background in the language(s) you are translating and good written and oral communication skills in both English and the language(s) are necessary.

Show Me the Money: $$$

You can charge by the word ($0.05 to $1.00), by the page ($7 to $20), per project, and by the hour ($30 to $50) or a per call flat fee ($50 to $175). Most translators make anywhere from $40,000 to $85,000 annually.

Business Equipment: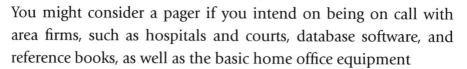

You might consider a pager if you intend on being on call with area firms, such as hospitals and courts, database software, and reference books, as well as the basic home office equipment

Business Base: 🏠

This is strictly an at-home business, unless you work for other companies, such as the courts, lawyers, hospitals, or other firms needing interpretations of other languages.

Clientele: 🗣

There is no set group for this business.

Starting Point: 🔑

You can translate writing material through the freelance Web sites found at the beginning of this chapter. If you are interested in working as a translator for area firms, contact them directly, leaving your name and contact information.

With local firms this will not be a constant job unless you live in an area where there is a large population of groups speaking other languages, but you can be on call with these organizations in the event a translator is needed.

Learn More:

Online

Things to know if you want to become a translator are at **www. scatia.org/infopage.htm.**

Info on getting started as a translator can be found at **www.gally. net/translation/gettingstarted.htm.**

Become a certified translator at **www.translatortips.net.**

Books

A Practical Guide for Translators (Topics in Translation, 13) by Geoffrey Samuelsson-Brown.

The Translator's Handbook by Morry Sofer.

Becoming a Translator: An Introduction to the Theory and Practice of Translation by Douglas H. Robinson.

Vacation Rental Agent: ☆ ☆ ☆

Do you know the best locations to vacation to? Have you been to many tourist destinations and have an understanding of what a vacation entails? Do not disregard the notion of being an expert in this area and offering your service for a fee. Not everyone has the time to research places abroad and find the best deals on hotels, car rental, the best areas to go, and so on.

Business Overview:

Research and find the best deals for your clients in the areas of:

- Airfare
- Boat/vehicle rentals
- Hotel Accomodations
- Dinning facilities
- Car rentals
- Night life/event festivities

You may also be asked to book the accommodations and write an itinerary of events with maps and other helpful resources for a week or two-week vacation.

Education/Skills:

Knowledge of the necessities individuals need for a relaxing vacation, an understanding of other places, and the resources a tourist might need will be helpful.

Show Me the Money: $$

You can charge a per project fee of $50 to $200 or a percentage of the cost of the vacation, as event or wedding planners do. Vacation rental agents make anywhere from $20,000 to $50,000 annually.

Business Equipment:

You will need good database software to keep the information on vacation spots and reference books on vacation destinations and hot spots.

Business Base:

This is strictly an at-home business.

Clientele:

Vacation seekers will be your main clients.

Starting Point:

Provide a Web site with vacation information and photos, offer clients a weekly or monthly newsletter filled with information about airfare specials or hotel specials for various destinations.

For example: The May issue of your newsletter might be focused on the islands of St. Thomas. You would include the current cruise lines that have included St. Thomas as a destination with coupons or discounts, as well as airfare and the island's tourism and festivities list.

You could contact cruise lines, hotels, and air line companies to announce your new services, to see what type of discounts they can offer your clients, and to see about a possible affiliation with their company.

Learn More:

Online

Vacation Rental Resources at **www.vacationrentalresources.com.**

A handful of vacation rental resources are available at **http://www. vrbo.com/global/links.htm.**

Virtual Assistant: ★ ★ ★ ★

Do you have a secretarial background? Do you know the basics of secretarial work, but are tired of traveling to an office everyday to provide that? You can now do this work from home.

Business Overview:

Provide secretarial services such as:

- Typing services
- Database administration
- Writing and editorial services

- Answering calls or making business calls

- Scheduling and arranging business meetings

Education/Skills:

A secretarial education or background would be helpful, along with good customer service skills.

Show Me the Money: $$$

Virtual assistants can charge an hourly rate of $20 to $40, a per project fee of $100 to $600, making an annual income of anywhere from $30,000 to $50,000.

Business Equipment:

Database software, scheduling, or calendar software will be needed.

Business Base:

This is an at-home business, with the option of offering in office services on a temporary basis to small businesses or other firms that need a secretary for startup, relief of their regular secretary, or for busy periods.

Clientele:

Any business or firm that hires secretaries or obtains secretarial work, students in need of typing services, or research staff in need of typing services will make up the biggest portion of your clientele.

Starting Point:

Contact small businesses and firms in your area announcing your service; offer your services to nonprofits for a fraction of the cost or give away a free week of your services to local firms.

Provide a Web site that includes your bio, services, and pricing, along with your contact information.

Learn More:

Online

Assist U (**www.assistu.com**) trains virtual assistants, and provides referrals to those who want to work with a virtual assistant.

Information on becoming a virtual assistant is available at **http:// www.va-theseries.com.**

Virtual assistance information and referrals can be found at **http:// www.assistu.com/va/va_how.shtml.**

Books

2-Second Commute: Join the Exploding Ranks of Freelance Virtual Assistants by Christine Durst, Michael Haaren.

Virtual Assistant, The Series: Become a Highly Successful, Sought After VA by Diana Ennen, Kelly Poelker.

The Virtual Assistant's Guide to Marketing by Michelle Jamison.

Voice-Over Actor: ☆ ☆ ☆

Do you enjoy acting? Want a way to get into acting without all the red tape and years of waiting to catch a break? Do you have a clear, crisp voice that is unique by nature?

Business Overview:

Provide voice recordings for material provided by your clients.

Education/Skills:

Good communication and oral skills are a must.

Show Me the Money: $$$$

Voice actors can make an hourly rate of $50 to $85, a per project fee of $125 to $1,000, and sometimes more depending on the project and the scope of the project, amounting to an annual rate of $50,000 to $150,000 or more.

Business Equipment:

Audio recording equipment, recording equipment, headphones, music, microphone, and a digital and analog mixer will be needed, along with the basic home-office equipment

Business Base:

This is partly a home-based business, but you may have to go into other professional recording studios and acting studios.

Clientele:

Audio book recording companies, commercials, directors, and producers will seek your services.

Starting Point:

Find auditions with any of the following audition sites and check for updates of new jobs in the industry:

www.auditionfinder.com	www.auditiontoday.com
www.backstage.com	www.castingaudition.com
www.castingdaily.com	www.castingyou.com
www.stagesource.com	www.castnet.com
www.employnow.com	www.exploretalent.com

www.productionhub.com   www.theauditiondatabase.com

www.musicaltheateraudition.com

Learn More:

Online

The site **www.voiceacting.com** answers questions on just about everything related to voice acting and voice-overs.

Books

The Voice Actor's Guide to Home Recording by Jeffrey P. Fisher, Harlan Hogan.

Secrets of Voice-Over Success: Top Voice-Over Actors Reveal How They Did It by Joan Baker.

There's Money Where Your Mouth Is: An Insider's Guide to a Career in Voice-Overs by Elaine A. Clark.

Webmaster: ★ ★ ★ ★

Some people are not sure what the difference between a Webmaster and a Web designer is; these are two very different services. While a Web designer creates a Web site for individuals, a Webmaster maintains and continuously updates information on a daily or weekly basis. Some Webmasters also work as contractors, where they find and hire individuals to do various jobs associated with the Web site's design and maintenance.

Business Overview:

Maintain Web site's information and various aspects of the Web site.

Education/Skills:

Understanding Web hosting procedures and Web design programs will be helpful. Although you will not be designing the program, you will need to use a Web designing program to update the site.

Show Me the Money: $$$$

Webmasters can charge an hourly rate of $30 to $50 or a weekly rate of $200 to $800. Depending on how many clients they can handle on a weekly basis, Webmasters can make anywhere from $40,000 to $100,000 or more annually.

Business Equipment:

You should have high-speed Internet, a Web design program, coding software, database software, and reference books.

Business Base:

This is strictly an at-home business.

Clientele:

There is no set group of clientele for this business, but Web site owners, businesses, and firms looking to have a Web site produced will make up the majority of your clients.

Starting Point:

You can find work from the freelance boards that were provided at the beginning of this chapter. You can also contact Web designers who do not have an affiliation with other Webmasters and create a business affiliation relationship with them.

Learn More:

Online

Webmaster Resources are at **www.webmasters-resources.com.**

Helping webmasters and DMOZ editors alike to improve Web sites by providing resources at **www.dmoz-resources.com/zone.**

Online tools for Webmasters and Web designers can be found at **www.webmaster-toolkit.com.**

Books

Teach Yourself How to Become a Webmaster in 14 Days (Sams Teach Yourself) by James L. Mohler.

Webmastering for Dummies by Daniel A. Tauber, Brenda Kienan.

Webmasters' Secret Internet Marketing & Search Engine Positioning Strategies by Bannin K. Lary.

Web Designer: ☆ ☆ ☆ ☆

Do you enjoy designing Web pages and e-commerce sites? Do you understand the mechanics behind creating a Web site from the ground up? Web designers have a tough job on their hands; they must be articulate, creative, and able to handle the pressure and challenges associated with the business.

Business Overview:

Design Web sites with animation, flash, and e-commerce.

Education/Skills:

An understanding of Web design and search engine mechanics are a basic requirement for this business.

Show Me the Money: $$$$

You can charge anywhere from $300 to $1,200 per Web site. You can also charge an hourly rate of $35 to $50, making on average of $35,000 to $150,000 annually.

Business Equipment:

Web design programs and software, graphic design programs, Web optimization programs, flash and animation programs and software, a good computer with high RAM, a top of the line modem, an excellent graphics card, and memory to spare are necessary. In addition, high-speed Internet will be helpful.

Business Base:

This is strictly an at-home business.

Clientele:

There is no set group for this business.

Starting Point:

Provided in the Learn More section, you can find work to bid on right away. You can also create an affiliate relationship with Webmasters.

Learn More:

Online

Visit **http://www.findwebdesigners.net**.

Books

How to Start a Home-Based Web Design Business, 3rd (Home-Based Business Series) by Jim Smith.

SUCCESS STORY: MIKE'S LOCK & SAFE, INC.

Michael Leach founded Mike's lock & Safe, Inc. in 1982. After working in a hardware store out of high school he secured a job in a wholesale hardware and locksmith supply warehouse. It was after he moved from California to Oregon to work for a locksmith company he realized it was time to make the move to entrepreneurship.

SUCCESS STORY: MIKE'S LOCK & SAFE, INC.

"I realized I would have to work for myself in order to get anywhere in this field and keep my sanity and make a few dollars for myself," he said.

Without a business degree he has successfully maintained and operated Mike's Lock & Safe, Inc., along with his wife, for 25 years.

His business	24-hour locksmith service.
How his idea was sparked	I learned quickly that this business breeds a nasty form of ownership. Employees were often mistreated money- and overtime-wise, and after having been stiffed for 204 hours of overtime by the guy in Oregon I worked two years for, I decided I could go out and make $5.37 an hour on my own. I made the move six months later, one month after my first son was born, a pretty risky move looking back on it.
Why he started his own business	My type A personality was one I knew would require me to be my own boss if I wanted things done right. Trying to be perfect all the time was a curse even through school.
The pros and cons	Pro: Watching my wife and our three boys stand tall and tell their friends about how their husband/dad started his own business and see the pride in their faces when they tell them about it. Con: Having been the ONLY night call person for 25 years. It gets tougher to drag myself out of bed at three in the morning or four times in a night and then still get up and go to work on time the next day the older I get.
Type of business	We have a storefront and always have. I did run the business from home one month while waiting for a space to open up and found that it was very easy to do from home also. I just feel the customer will treat a security-type business with more respect if it has its own storefront.
In his first few years of business	My wife had our first boy in September of 1982. I started my business in October of 1982. My wife went back to work after maternity leave and worked the first year and a half of our son's life, during the initial growth of the company.

SUCCESS STORY: MIKE'S LOCK & SAFE, INC.

	So, my only concern was to get her out of that insurance claims job and home as fast as possible. It took 18 months of working hard to get to the point where she could her give notice and come home to raise our first child and the two that followed
He saw a steady flow of income in...	The first three years actually were steady as they improved, but we were having children during that time and those little buggers aren't cheap. It wasn't until the end of the third year when we saw the company had tripled in gross income that we realized we were going to do just fine.
His likes and dislikes about running a business	LOVE: We became comfortable enough to experiment with other types of businesses. The fact that my wife and I can do this together makes it worth the effort. DISLIKE: Still doing 24-hour service after 25 years and my body is telling me STOP, I NEED MORE REST NOW!
His personal qualities that have helped her in her business endeavors	I never considered myself an outgoing person, but apparently was better than I realized. Customers said the way I deal with the public so easily and my ability to make them feel appreciated and like family was the biggest factor in being so devoted to always calling me back when needed. I'd call it more of being a chatterbox.
What he thinks it takes to be successful	That's easy, LOTS and LOTS of patience and sacrifice by not only you, but also your wife and friends, if any.
Future aspirations for his business	Hard to say; we both have so many ideas of what we want to do now that we are approaching the dreaded 50-year-old mark (I'll be 49 this August and she'll be 47 in November). We hope to buy some land later this year (been looking for a year) and work on making it a place we can retire. We are looking for a place for our dog washing/grooming business and a larger place will also help raise abandoned dogs and find homes for them, while grooming and improving their eating habits. That, or

SUCCESS STORY: MIKE'S LOCK & SAFE, INC.	
	winning one of the screenwriting contests and selling a script to show I can actually write something worthy of consideration. I am also an emerging screenwriter.
The key to his success	The key to my success was also my biggest downfall. I was so obsessed with the notion that my customers would leave if I took time off that after 15 years I had only taken two vacations. Being available when others were not, certainly helped me get well known. The past 10 years, I've tried harder to take more vacations, but still miss a year sporadically due to my effort to be available.
A challenge he faced while running her business	I never really had any issues other than refusing to raise my prices until 15 years later; I lost $7,000 after grossing over $100,000. Just learning to do what's right for me, as well as the customer, so we don't have to always cut back at home. Otherwise, it would have to be the fact I've never missed a day of work. I've suffered three concussions during my work, one where I was hit and pinned between two vehicles, but I managed to push the other car off me, multiple broken or separated ribs due to overwork and lack of rest. I've had torn muscles in my drilling shoulder multiple times and pelvic hernia for 15 years.
	I'd say just dealing with everyday issues no matter how bad, and working through them, to support my family.
His advice to potential business owners	Do NOT let the customer dictate your life and make you feel you can't close the shop when you feel you need some rest. Make sure you raise your prices when necessary and don't be afraid to take TIME OFF each year to help heal your body for the next year's work ahead.
His Business Day	In my youth (24-36) I worked 12 to 14 hour days Monday through Friday. Saturday was 9 hours and Sunday was usually 3 to 4. In total, 72 to 81 hours a week EVERY WEEK. From 37 to 45 it dropped about 10 hours a week as I learned to slow down. And by 46, I realized that 45 to 55 hour weeks were all that I wanted to do in order to heal up for the next week's work.

SUCCESS STORY: MIKE'S LOCK & SAFE, INC.

The ease of breaking into his industry	Depends on the building you want me to break into? (Sorry, locksmith humor.) It's easy to break into, but only if you realize that it is NOT a career that pays well working for others.
His most embarrassing moment	That would have to be during ownership of my sports card and comic shop. I loved taking on the additional challenge of putting on those sports card convention events; they take an enormous amount of money, time, and effort to put together. It gave Craig (an employee) and I a thrill to use Craig's connections to get real pro players to come sign autographs for the kids. (Craig was the towel boy for the Portland Beavers Triple A baseball team.) I would host these events, and on the last one I held, we used the largest place we were lucky enough to find available on our timeline, the Tigard High school cafeteria with a stage. What I didn't expect was the janitor coming in, just as we opened the doors to the anxious public (and with 27 other shop owners and collectors tables ready and waiting inside) to come to the stage and set up a microphone for us, and tell me that we can use it to introduce the players if we wanted. I was not prepared to do that, but thought okay, I'll go up early and try it out. When I finished all my chores of greeting the flood of early customers, I went up without any thought, and started to explain what was in store for everyone when the players arrived. As I began, I realized I really didn't know what I wanted to say and began a broken batch of information, finally apologizing for the lack of prep and excused myself back to the shop tables again. Everyone of course knew me, so I got ribbed a lot by the people that actually saw it. ("Hey Mike, do you have a Ken Grif, Grif, Griffey Jr. card?")

Success Story: Mike's Lock & Safe, Inc.

	Fortunately, Craig tried to help me on the next try and after his totally freezing once up there, I was able to go save him and enjoy bantering my usual mumbo jumbo without hesitation, to the delight of the shoppers. (It helped to see Craig do worse than my first effort.)
	It was the biggest success I had in any of my convention efforts, in spite of my lack of prep to announce things and the ribbing we got for weeks to follow.
His most bizarre request	I had a call at 1:35 a.m. asking how much and how fast I could get to them to unlock four pairs of handcuffs. The guy's story went like this: My naked wife is handcuffed to the bedposts and I need a locksmith. I countered sorry, that has liability and lawsuit written all over it. We bantered back and forth for 25 minutes (he wasn't taking no for an answer, but he was nice about it, just pleading and pathetic sounding) when I finally told him if I couldn't hand him my bolt cutters and get time to get a witness to ride with me, and let him cut them all off and bring them back to me in the van outside, then I couldn't help him.
	He claimed he wasn't willing to cut them off and promised to throw a towel over her to make sure I wasn't at risk. I finally, realizing I was getting nowhere and was tired, told the man politely that my career wasn't worth being thrown in jail because he couldn't part with four pairs of $16 dollar handcuffs. I said sorry and hung up.

Chapter 4

Businesses You Can Start For Between $500 And $1,000

"Eighty percent of success is showing up."

-*Woody Allen*

Animal Breeder: ✫ ✫ ✫

Do you love animals? Whether you are interested in dogs or cats, birds or gerbils, or even horses you can be a certified breeder if you have enough land and enough patience.

Business Overview:

Take care of and mate animals and sell the babies. This can be a rewarding job for any animal lover. Some animals can only be mated once a year and will only provide one or two babies to sell. You will need to understand how to administer shots to the animals or hire a veterinarian to care for the animals.

Education/Skills:

You should have knowledge of the various breeds of animals and how to care for their young, as well as when and how shots and other special care should be given and the behavior of animals and their children.

Show Me the Money: $$$

Depending on the type of animals you breed and how many varieties you have you can make anywhere from $15,000 to $50,000 annually. To add more income you can also add Dog/animal Trainer to this profession and make an additional $40,000 to $60,000.

Business Equipment: 📱 ☎ 📄 💿 🖥 🌓 🗖

You will need animal care products, a variety of kennels, and preferably a large barn for this business.

Business Base: 🏠

This is strictly an at-home business.

Clientele: 🐾

There is no set clientele group, other than animal lovers.

Starting Point: 🔑

Purchase one set of animals and mate them. You can begin working your way up after you have sold that set of animals. Each time the mother is pregnant advertise in local papers.

Learn More:

Online

Exotic animal breeders' resources at **www.exoticanimalbreeders.net.**

National Association for Animal Breeders at **www.naab-css.org.**

Animal Trainer : ☆ ☆ ☆

Have you ever seen the dogs or animals on TV who can do sophisticated tricks or obey on command? Think Benji, Lassie, or Mr. Ed.

Business Overview:

Provide round the clock training camps at two-week intervals. You can provide them every two months, every other month to allow for breaks, or continuously. To train animals accurately they will need to have training day and night; this could be a family business where you and your spouse take shifts. For additional income you can add Animal Breeder to this profession.

Education/Skills:

Knowledge of animal behavior and training knowledge are imperative.

Show Me the Money: $$$

You can charge anywhere from $200 to $500 per animal for the two-week period and make $40,000 to $75,000 annually.

Business Equipment: 📱 ☎ 📄 💿 🖥 🌙 ▭

Dog training equipment, cages, and animal sleeping quarters will be needed.

Business Base: 🏠

If you have enough land and sleeping quarters this can strictly be an at-home business.

Clientele: 💬

Animal lovers will seek your services.

Starting Point: 🔒

Contact veterinarians and vet hospitals in your area to offer your services to their clients. Get involved with nonprofit animal rescue centers. Train a dog that is up for adoption at the humane society for free, and then contact the media and ask them for help adopting him, showing a short piece on his training to help him find a home. This will give your company media attention and get an animal a home; you could do this monthly or yearly.

Learn More

Online

Become a professional animal trainer or behaviorist by just completing these courses available at **www.animalschool.net.**

The site **www.animalbehaviorcollege.com** offers dog training schools and animal trainer jobs.

Animal Behavior Society at **www.animalbehavior.org.**

National Association of Dog Obedience Instructors (NADOI) at **www.nadoi.org.**

Books

Careers with Animals: Exploring Occupations Involving Dogs, Horses, Cats, Birds, Wildlife, and Exotics by Ellen Shenk.

Kicked, Bitten, and Scratched: Life and Lessons at the World's Premier School for Exotic Animal Trainers by Amy Sutherland.

Animal Training: Successful Animal Management Through Positive Reinforcement by Ken Ramirez (Editor).

Answering Service: ★ ★ ★

Businesses do not always want their clients to talk to an answering machine after hours or on the weekends. Therefore, they hire an answering service to take care of their customers during those hours.

Business Overview:

Answering services answer calls for businesses, doctors' offices, dentists, or other healthcare professionals in the evenings or on the weekends. Primary duties include:

- Answer calls

- Answer common questions regarding the business

- Page a business rep in case of an emergency

- Take messages for the business

- Write daily reports about the callers or calls received

Education/Skills:

Customer service and telephone operating skills are a must. Good phone etiquette is also extremely important.

Show Me the Money: $$$

Depending on your clientele you can make $30,000 to $60,000 annually. You should charge a monthly fee and a per-call rate, or you can contact local answering services in your area to see how much they charge.

Business Equipment:

You will need a multi-line phone with a switchboard, billing, database, and bookkeeping software, and call service software or scripts.

Business Base:

This is primarily at-home. Many answering services have grown to need additional employees and office space, depending on the amount of clients you have.

Clientele: 🐾

Doctors, lawyers, dentists, or other private practice healthcare professionals and local business owners will seek your services.

Starting Point: 🔓

Contact a local healthcare professional and ask if you can offer your service free of charge for a month. After the month is up you can ask them to evaluate your service, and you can send them detailed information on using your service in the future.

Learn More:

Online

Information on how to start an answering service business can be found at **www.startananansweringservice.com**.

Information and resources on the answering service industry can be found at **www.answerconnect.com/educational-info**.

Books

Internet Marketing For Your Answering Services Business by James Orr and Jassen Bowman

How to Start and Manage an Answering Service Business by Jerre G. Lewis.

Automotive Detailer: ★ ★ ★

Love to see cars shined up, rolling down the street with neon lights, cool logos, or artwork displayed on the hood or sides of a car? Love to be able to do that and make money, too?

Business Overview:

Auto detailing can range from airbrushing images, names, and logos on cars and trucks to applying tinted windows and customary window art.

Education/Skills:

You should have some type of auto detailing background or education. If not, take a course supplied by adult education programs or local colleges.

Show Me the Money: $$$

Your earnings could be anywhere between $30,000 and $60,000 annually, charging $100 to $500 per job. If you add bodywork and restoration, you can make an additional $40,000 to $50,000 annually.

Business Equipment:

A variety of paint supplies and an airbrush system, brushes, car detail equipment, sanding equipment, supplies for window tinting and art, and a variety of car stencils will be helpful.

Business Base:

If you live in a residential neighborhood, you might not be able to get a license to provide these services. Check with your state and county to see if you are zoned to provide this service. Links are provided in the following section. If you cannot get a license, you will need to work out of your garage or other body shop.

Clientele:

There is no set clientele group.

Starting Point:

Detail a friend's car or your own to show off your skills. You should also apply your number to the design, as this will provide advertising for you. You can also contact small garages to see if they have detailing services. If they do not, ask if they would be interested in affiliating services.

Learn More:

Online

Auto detailing training, news, resources, and expert advice offered for consumers and do-it-yourself detailers can be found at **www.autodetail-school.com**.

Books

Start Your Own Automobile Detailing Business by Eileen Figure Sandlin.

Auto Detail Pro (3 Disc Set) DVD.

Automotive Detailing: A Complete Car Guide for Auto Enthusiasts and Detailing Professionals by Don Taylor.

Ultimate Auto Detailing Projects by David H Jacobs Jr.

Business Broker: ★ ★

Do you enjoy the real estate market, but with a business flare? Then you will love being a business broker. A business broker becomes involved when a person wants to start a business and is leaning toward preexisting businesses.

Business Overview:

A business broker works as the liaison between the owner selling the business and the potential buyer. Just as a real estate agent is to the housing market, a business broker is to the business market.

Education/Skills:

In some states you may need a real estate license. Check with your state to see if this or other certificates are required. You should understand sales and perhaps have a background in business; it would be wise to at least understand sales.

Show Me the Money: $$$$

A business broker usually takes about 10 to 15 percent of the sale. Depending on how much business you can obtain you can make up to $100,000 annually.

Business Equipment:

You will need software that provides business and/or legal documents so you do not have to use the services of a lawyer. You may also need additional software for letterheads and correspondence.

Business Base:

This is an at-home business with some travel time, averaging about 40 percent for meetings, final sales, and other face-to-face business dealings.

Clientele:

Your clientele are business owners looking to retire or sell their business.

Starting Point:

A good starting point would be to search through local listings of businesses for sale. Contact the owners and inform them about the type of business you are starting. Ask if you can take on the sale of their business for a small percentage. Ask for 5 percent of the sale just to get your foot in the door and to get yourself established.

Learn More:

Online

Business Insight and business resource software can be found at http://www.brs-inc.com.

Caterer: ★ ★ ★

Do you love cooking, but do not want to answer to anyone other than yourself? Catering can be a fulfilling home business if you love to prepare food and feed others.

Business Overview:

When you become a caterer your basic responsibility will be to cook, deliver, serve, and clean up at events you have been hired to cater. You will also need to speak to clients on a regular basis to be sure everything is in order, the head count is correct, and the food items you will be serving are correct.

Education/Skills:

Food preparation and culinary skills are necessary. No culinary degree is required, but it might come in handy when you are first starting out. It is important to know the basics of cooking and seasoning.

Show Me the Money: $$$$

Most caterers charge a per plate fee around $8.00. You can also charge per project fees. A caterer can make up to $100,000 annually if they are well known in their community and have good word of mouth advertising.

Business Equipment: 📱 ☎ 📄 💿 🖥 ☽

Beyond the normal business equipment needed for a home

business, you will also need a large van to carry your equipment and food and culinary equipment, such as pans, warmers, and utensils.

Business Base:

If you have a large enough kitchen, this could primarily be at-home, but if not you may need to rent kitchen space. If it were home-based, this would be about 50 percent travel time, which includes the serving of the food.

Clientele:

Your clientele is very large, as the majority of people have some form of catered event at least once, if not a few times, throughout their lives. You can offer your services to all events or focus on weddings and showers.

Starting Point:

Contact local churches or charitable organizations to see if you can cater an event for a fraction of the cost. Produce business cards to be left at the event or you can offer the food and the preparation of the food as a donation. This will give you a good clientele base to start off with.

Learn More:

Online

Complete online resource at **http://www.startcatering.com/**.

Online database of catering, chef, and hospitality jobs are available at **http://www.caterer.com.**

Books

How to Start a Home-Based Catering Business by Denise Vivaldo.

The Food Service Professional Guide to Successful Catering: Managing the Catering Operation for Maximum Profit by Sony Bode.

Catering like a Pro: From Planning to Profit by Francine Halvorsen.

Child-Care Provider: ✯ ✯ ✯

A child-care provider offers clients a safe and friendly atmosphere for their children while the client is working or studying at school. If you love children and have a home large enough, a fenced-in backyard, and a suitable environment, child care would be a great business venture for you.

Business Overview:

You will watch and care for a number of different children during the week or during the hours you and your client have agreed upon.

Your responsibilities include:

- Watching the child
- Feeding the child
- Teaching the child
- Disciplining the child
- Keeping a daily schedule
- Daily care (brushing teeth, diaper changing, and so on)

There may be other responsibilities included with children who have special needs. You should be sure to have the parents sign a variety of papers concerning the schedule you have set for the day-care, the rules and the consequences that their child will endure if they break the rules, and other important forms, such as medical emergency forms.

Education/Skills:

Depending on where you live you may need a day-care license to open a business. A representative may have to come out to your home to see that it is suited for children. It will be helpful to be CPR certified, which only takes a day or two if you take a workshop.

Show Me the Money: $$

You can start out charging around $60 a week per child. That could be more for special needs children. Many childcare providers make $30,000 to $60,000 annually.

Business Equipment:

You will need playground equipment placed in your backyard and a fence that surrounds the playground equipment. With some children you might need a variety of home child-proofing equipment for safety.

Business Base:

This is strictly an at-home business.

Clientele:

Your clientele will be working parents.

Starting Point:

You could start by putting a small ad in local papers, watch the children of your relatives, or make a sign to put in your front yard that indicates you are a child-care provider.

Learn More:

Online

Child-care Provider information can be found at **http://home. ivillage.com/homeoffice/homeoff/0,,80wt-3,00.html.**

Books

How to Open & Operate a Financially Successful Child Care Service: With Companion CD-ROM by Tina Musial.

How to Start a Home-Based Day-Care Business, 4th (Home-Based Business Series) by Shari Steelsmith.

Family Child Care Contracts and Policies: How to Be Businesslike in a Caring Profession (Redleaf Press Business Series) by Tom Copeland.

Consignment Shop Owner: ★ ★

People grow out of their clothes constantly and for those who do not like garage sales, what do they do with their outdated clothes? They usually go to consignment shops or thrift stores.

Business Overview:

Running a consignment shop means you will need to rent a storefront somewhere in your city, preferably a thriving area. You will have to obtain your goods by having clothing drives or advertising the acceptance of clothes. Many consignment shop owners purchase clothes that are free of stains and rips for a small fee from clients, and then they increase the price when they put it on the racks to sell. You can also have others sell their clothes on your racks while you earn a 40 to 50 percent commission on all sales, which will pay for the time on the shelves, labor, and the cost of the storefront.

Education/Skills:

You should understand the day-to-day operations of running a business, but other than that knowledge you need no additional degrees or skills.

Show Me the Money: $$

Your net income will range anywhere from $30,000 to $50,000, depending on the area your storefront is in, store hours, and advertising.

Business Equipment:

Clothing racks, cash register, counter space, a steam cleaner (to clean all the clothes that come in before they hit the racks) and other display equipment will be needed.

Business Base:

This is strictly a storefront business, with barely any home time.

Clientele:

Individuals interested in purchasing consignment shop clothes, mostly families with lower incomes, will be your main clients.

Starting Point:

Put together a clothing drive in which you offer part of your proceeds to area homeless shelters. Rent a small flea market space and begin selling the clothes you received from the clothing drive until you raise enough capital to open your storefront continue with weekend or weekday flea markets.

Learn More:

Although there are a number of consignment shops worldwide, such as Goodwill and the Salvation Army, there are very few resources for this business.

Computer Repair Specialist: ★ ★ ★

If you enjoy fixing and working with computers and know the

mechanics of doing this, running a computer repair shop would be a perfect business for you. Computer repair specialists, especially those who do home visits, are needed everywhere. Many people find it cost effective to have their current systems fixed as opposed to buying an entirely new system.

Business Overview:

A computer repair specialist should be available to do any of the following services:

- Troubleshoot small errors

- Remove and install new hard drives

- Install additional memory

- Removal of viruses

- Data recovery, full system recovery, and back up of data

- Network and modem problems

- Installing additional hard drives, zip drives, or DVD/CD readers/writers

- Installing software

- Cleaning the computer system

There may be additional computer services that you could provide, such as setting up computers, printers, and networking equipment for small businesses.

Education/Skills:

Knowledge of computer hardware and repair and a background and education in computer repair is required.

Show Me the Money: $$$

Computer repair technicians, especially those on call, can make a great living by charging anywhere from $40 to $75 an hour. Many computer specialists make between $50,000 to $100,000.

Business Equipment:

Computer repair equipment, extra equipment, cleaning tools, and reference books, along with the basic home office equipment, will be needed.

Business Base:

This is both an at-home and a travel business, although you may find yourself out of the home office more often. It should be close to 60 percent travel time and 40 percent office time. But if you offer assistance over the phone the time spent traveling could change.

Clientele:

There is no set group for this business. Anyone who owns a computer needs it fixed once in a while, and with over 300 million homes and businesses in the United States with computers you will have all the clients you need.

Starting Point:

You might begin by fixing a friend's or family member's computer. Consider creating a Web site and advertising your services there.

Learn More:

Online

Technibble.com is a free resource for computer technicians.

Guide to troubleshooting and repairing computers can be found at **www.daileyint.com/hmdpc/manual.htm**.

Books

Start Your Own Computer Business: Building a Successful PC Repair and Service Business by Supporting Customers and Managing Money by Morris Rosenthal, Reva Rubenstein.

Computer Repair with Diagnostic Flowcharts: Troubleshooting PC Hardware Problems from Boot Failure to Poor Performance by Morris Rosenthal.

Desktop Publisher: ✮ ✮ ✮ ✮

Desktop publishing combines design and writing services in one and allows the desktop publisher to provide a variety of different services.

Business Overview:

Desktop publishers are familiar with and are able to provide a variety of periodicals and materials such as:

- Flyers
- Pamphlets
- Brochures
- Books
- Newsletters
- Ebooks

Depending on your client's needs you may be hired to do other, yet similar, jobs.

Education/Skills:

Design and writing skills are a must; you should also have good communication and editorial skills, be familiar with typesetting and the printing process, and have good knowledge of desktop publishing software.

Show Me the Money: $$$$

Desktop publishers make anywhere from $40,000 to $100,000 annually, charging $35 to $50 hourly or $75 to $800 per project.

Business Equipment:

You will need graphic design software, desktop publishing software, Web design software, photo editing software, a variety of clip art and royalty free photos, a digital camera, a top of the line printer, and a variety of printing paper.

Business Base:

This is strictly an at-home business.

Clientele:

There is no set group for this business.

Starting Point:

Put together a Web site offering your services and a portfolio of your work. Try the freelance job boards provided earlier for work.

Learn More:

Online

Extensive desktop and electronic publishing resource — **www. desktoppublishing.com**.

Learn how to do graphic design, desktop publishing, and typography. Explore terms and techniques at **www.desktoppub. about.com**.

Books

How to Start a Home-Based Desktop Publishing Business, 3rd by Louise Kursmark.

Desktop Publishing StyleGuide by Sandra Lentz Devall.

Looking Good in Print by Roger Parker.

Disc Jockey: ☆ ☆

Love to play music? There is nothing like making sure the music is playing and the party, event, or wedding guests are on the dance floor enjoying that music. This job has two options:

First Option — As a regular disc jockey

Second Option — As a disc jockey with karaoke abilities

Offering karaoke will help your business grow, create additional income, and give you the option of offering one or both services to your public, local clubs, bar owners, and other events.

Business Overview:

Play continuous music and offer entertainment for weddings, local events, catered events, birthday parties, and so forth.

Education/Skills:

A love for music, good communication skills, and some rhythm are all you need.

Show Me the Money: $$$

DJs make between $75 and $250 per night and $30,000 to $60,000 annually.

Business Equipment: 📱 ☎ 📄 💿 🖥 🌙 📇

Turntables, a large collection of music, mixers, a Karaoke machine, Karaoke style music, microphones, and theatrical lighting will be needed.

Business Base:

This is a traveling business; merely 20 percent of your time will be at your in-home office.

Clientele:

There is no set group for this business.

Starting Point:

Offer your services at a low rate for local events, especially ones that will have media attention. Sign up with Web sites and various DJ service sites and get an affiliation with an event planner or wedding planner in your area.

Learn More:

Online—Disc Jockey

Disc jockey resources are at **http://www.discjockeyonline.com/**.

Find resources, tools, and put your name into a DJ search for clients in your area at **http://www.djsourceonline.com/**.

Complete resources for today's DJs is available at **http://www. discjockey101.com.**

The site **http://www.djfinder.com/** helps bring together DJs and event planners.

Books—Disc Jockey

The Mobile DJ Handbook: How to Start and Run a Profitable Mobile Disc Jockey Service by Stacy Zemon.

How to DJ Right: The Art and Science of Playing Records by Frank Broughton, Bill Brewster.

Intellect: Techno House Progressive (2003) Starring: Various Artists DVD.

Online—Karaoke

Karaoke software and resources available at **www.unifykaraoke. com/english/karaoke_business.htm.**

Karaoke systems and equipment at **www.karaoke2go.com.**

Books—Karaoke

Karaoke Capitalism: Daring to Be Different in a Copycat World by Jonas Ridderstrale, Kjell A. Nordstrom.

Inspirational Speaker: ★ ★ ★

Do you have a personal experience that has made you a better person? Are you more successful, more productive and appreciative, kinder, and have the ability to look at life differently because of it? Or do you have a life path that you have taken that has made all your dreams come true?

Business Overview:

An inspirational or motivational speaker shares his or her experiences by traveling the world and speaking to the public on issues such as:

- Success

- Finding your life's path

- Addiction recovery

- Abuse or neglect recovery and forgiveness

- Path to happiness

These are only a few examples of issues and topics you could be speaking to a class or audience about.

Education/Skills:

Good communication skills are a must. A good sense of humor always helps and in-depth knowledge of the issues you are speaking about is necessary.

Show Me the Money: $$$

Inspirational speakers can make anywhere from $150 to $400 per class or session, sometimes more if you are well known. On average you can make around $30,000 to $90,000 annually.

Business Equipment:

If you will be using information, tables, graphs, or other such graphics with your presentation, you should have a projector and projector screen to cart to your speaking engagements. No other equipment is needed with this business.

Business Base:

This is mostly a traveling business; you may spend a mere 10 to 20 percent of your time in your office.

Clientele:

There is no set group for this business.

Starting Point:

To start out you can contact domestic violence shelters and see if you can offer your services to them for free or at a very low rate. If you are offering this service for free, do not forget to involve the media. You also can contact other motivational and inspirational speakers in your area to offer a day of inspiration, inviting people from shelters and other low-income families.

Learn More:

Online

Professional Motivational Keynote Speakers is at **www. professionalspeakerwebsite.com.**

Books

Speak Up With Confidence: A Step-By-Step Guide for Speakers and Leaders by Carol Kent.

Landscape Artist: ✰ ✰

If you enjoy working outside cutting lawns and landscaping, why not earn a living doing it?

Business Overview:

Your duties could entail:

- Cut the grass

- Trim the weeds

- Trim small branches on trees and bushes

- Raking the grass and excess weeds from the grass

- Blowing the excess grass from the driveway and walkway

- Landscaping the lawn with bushes, shrubs, and flowers

Your client may ask you to provide other duties, while other clients may not need all the services listed.

Education/Skills:

A love for beautifying neighborhoods is all you need.

Show Me the Money: $$$

You can charge an hourly rate of $35 to $60 or a per yard rate, which will have to be estimated based on the size and time it would take you to cut it. This could be anywhere between $65 to $300, with an annual income of $20,000 to $80,000.

Business Equipment:

A commercial lawnmower, a blower, hedge cutters, an edger, a weed whacker, rakes, and a truck or trailer to haul your equipment will be needed.

Business Base:

This is a traveling business. Merely 10 percent of work is done in your office.

Clientele:

There is no set group for this business; anyone with a yard is a potential customer.

Starting Point:

Advertise with local papers and contact small apartment complexes to offer your services for half off for one month. All apartments and businesses sub-contract their work to local lawn care providers.

Learn More:

Books

How to Start a Home-Based Landscaping Business, 5th (Home-Based Business Series) by Owen Dell.

New Complete Guide to Landscaping: Design, Plant, Build (Better Homes and Gardens) by Better Homes and Gardens.

Landscape Estimating Methods (Means Landscape Estimating) by Sylvia Hollman Fee.

Landscaping Your Home: Creative Ideas from America's Best Gardeners (Fine Gardening Design Guides) by Fine Gardening Editors.

Memory Movie Producer: ☆ ☆ ☆ ☆

Have you seen the photo slide shows at funerals, graduations, and other such events? Have you seen the effect they have on people? These photo slides tell a person's story through the pictures on the screen and the words in the music.

Business Overview:

Scan photos of your client or upload the pictures from a CD or digital memory card. Using the slide show software you will arrange the pictures, the transitions, and the music. Create a DVD file and burn that to a blank DVD. Design a cover label and a DVD cover.

Education/Skills:

Understanding copyright laws for photographs and music is very important. You can only use snapshot photos, unless you get signed permission to use photos from a professional photographer.

Every song needs to be paid for and downloaded for the purpose of the project and can only be used once. Sign up with a monthly subscription music site, but make sure the music you download from them can be used with third party programs.

You should also have an understanding of desktop publishing.

Show Me the Money: $$

Many movie producers charge a $25 setup fee, which covers the cost of the DVD, the printing of the labels, paper, and so on, and then add a $0.50 to $1.00 fee per picture and a $1.00 fee per song. Normally one song will cover between 25 and 30 pictures, as the pictures will stay on the screen for about 11 to 12 seconds with a two second transition. As a memory movie or photo slide show producer you can make $20,000 to $50,000 annually.

Business Equipment:

A top of the line scanner, printer, and computer with plenty of memory and a DVD burner, memory movie or slide show software, a digital camera and software that can edit pictures and photographs are necessary. Blank DVDs, empty DVD cases, paper to fit into the DVD case (you should use 24 lb. card stock paper or glossy 8x10 photo paper) and DVD labels are also needed, as well as software for creating DVD labels and DVD cases.

Software Suggestions:

Arcsoft (www.arcsoft.com): You can choose Showbiz, DVD Slideshow, or VideoImpression.

Photodex (http://www.photodex.com): Choose from Photo Pro Gold, Producer, or Standard. You can even try the software for free before you buy it at.

On **www.download.com** you can download fully-functional versions demos to try of some of the best slide show programs.

Expressit can also be downloaded free at **http://www.download.com/exPressit/3000-2130_4-10539970.html**. This is a great and easy to use program for designing DVDs and DVD labels.

Business Base:

This is strictly an at-home business.

Clientele: 🗨

There is no set group for this business.

Starting Point: 🔓

Get in touch with local schools in your area and see if you can offer your services to the graduating classes. Ask if you can send flyers to the school, giving them a discount for the service.

When you cover the entire graduating class you will have to work with the school's photographer, and you could also take digital photos of school events, such as football and basketball games, dances, the prom, homecoming, and other such events to make sure you have a picture of all the students. You could also go to the school for one day and snap pictures of all the seniors. Most funeral homes offer this service to their clients, but you can contact local funeral homes to see if they are sub-contracting this service. See if you can offer them a better price.

This is a relatively new field. No books or materials are available on this business. If you have any questions regarding this business, feel free to contact me directly at writing4peace@msn.com.

Massage Therapist: ★ ★

Are you one of those people who love to take the stress out of other people's lives? Is there magic in your hands? Then let that magic out on those who need it most.

Business Overview:

Provide massage therapy to clients.

Education/Skills:

An education or background in massage therapy is required, as well as an understanding of muscular tissue and the effects of massage therapy.

Show Me the Money: $$$

Massage therapists can make anywhere from $35 to $125 per hour, with an annual income of somewhere between $50,000 and $80,000.

Business Equipment:

Hot stones, warm clothes, soft, soothing music, and rubbing oils will be helpful.

Business Base:

Unless you have a separate room and live in a commercially zoned area, you might not get the okay to provide this service in your home. You can contact beauty salons and day spas to rent out a room or offer your services to their clients. You can always get a small storefront and sell relaxation products in the front with massage therapy in the back.

Clientele:

There is no set group for this business.

Starting Point:

As a freelance gig offer your services to those in your community who deserve some relaxation: teachers, service men and women, police officers, firefighters, volunteer workers, and the like.

Learn More:

Online

The American Massage Therapy Association (**www.amtamassage. org/becometherapist/intro.html**) offers massage therapy information and resources for AMTA.

The truth about becoming a massage therapist is available at **www. massagetherapycareers.com.**

Massage therapy training and schools can be found at **http://www. naturalhealers.com.**

Books

Deep Tissue Massage, Revised: A Visual Guide to Techniques by Art Riggs, Thomas W. Myers.

The Complete Guide to Massage: A Step-by-Step Approach to Total Body Relaxation by Susan Mumford.

Organizer: ★ ★ ★

Do you enjoy organizing things? Can you make things fit into little spaces and find a place for everything?

Business Overview:

Arrange, label, and organize clients' home offices, closets, or other rooms in their homes or businesses.

Education/Skills:

Good customer service skills and organizational skills are a must.

Show Me the Money: $$$

Professional organizers can charge a per hour fee of $25 to $45 or a per project fee (which would significantly depend on the project and room), and they usually make anywhere from $35,000 to $60,000 annually.

Business Equipment:

There is no other business equipment needed for this business. The client will need to purchase all the organizational equipment, or you can charge more for shopping and travel time.

Business Base:

With this business there will be more travel time than at-home time. Much of your time will be spent at your client's home or office.

Clientele:

There is no set group for this business.

Starting Point:

Develop a Web site with tips and tricks to staying organized. You can also offer a newsletter with coupons and time and money saving tips. Advertise on healthy living, small business, and busy moms sites, as these will be the majority of your clients.

Learn More:

Online

National Association of Professional Organizers at **www.napo-wi.com.**

How to start a professional closet organizing business and tips and resources for professionals can be found at **www.homebusinesscenter.com/articles/closet_organizer.html.**

Books

How to Start a Home-Based Professional Organizing Business (Home-Based Business Series) by Dawn Noble.

Everything You Need to Know about a Career as a Professional Organizer by Sara Pedersen.

Organizing Plain and Simple: A Ready Reference Guide with Hundreds of Solutions to Your Everyday Clutter Challenges by Donna Smallin.

A Manual for Professional Organizers by Cyndi Seidler.

The Beverly Hills Organizer's Home Organizing Bible: A Pro's Answers to Your Organizing Prayers by Linda Koopersmith.

Personal Chef: ✮ ✮

Cooking for a restaurant or other business can be grueling and time consuming, but when you are a personal chef you have more leniency when it comes to your time and what you will cook.

Business Overview: *

Cook for individuals at their home or at corporate events. You can also offer meals to families that are prepared and frozen, such as lasagna, chili, beef stew, chicken dishes, or other meals that can easily be baked for quick meals.

*To add extra money to this business you can also provide cake decorations. See Cake Decorating in Chapter 3.

Education/Skills:

Knowledge of cooking or a culinary degree is suggested.

Show Me the Money: $$$

Personal chefs can make anywhere from $30,000 to $60,000 annually. The amount you charge your client will depend on the meal cost, the quantity, and time spent preparing and cooking.

Business Equipment: 📱 ☎ 📄 💿 💻 🌙 🔁

You will need a variety of cooking utensils, pots, pans, and baking pans, an industrial size oven, and reference books or other materials.

If you will be delivering the food, you will need a small van to carry it, along with other carrying cases and products.

Business Base:

You will mostly spend your time away from home, especially if you will be cooking at meetings, events, and other people's homes.

Clientele:

Professionals in your area will seek your services.

Starting Point:

Offer your services to a family shelter or homeless shelter; a small shelter that houses only a few families at a time would be sufficient. Contact the local media to inform them of your intentions. Create a feed the hungry campaign in your local area and invite other chefs to get involved and cook meals for families at other area shelters.

You can also put together a Web site offering your services to the public. They can choose their food and meals from the site.

Learn More:
Online

Information on becoming a personal chef is available at **www.personalchefsnetwork.com/becoming_a_personal_chef.html**.

Comprehensive guide to personal chef services is at **www.articleinsider.com/article/175988**.

The best personal chef Web site solution can be found at **www.ezchef.net/becoming_a_personal_chef.html**.

Books

How to Start a Home-Based Personal Chef Business (Home-Based Business Series) by Denise Vivaldo.

How to Open & Operate a Financially Successful Personal Chef Business: With Companion CD-ROM from Atlantic Publishing.

Professional Photographer: ☆ ☆

Do you enjoy taking professional pictures of families, events, or buildings? You can make a decent living doing something you truly love.

Business Overview: *

Take photographs of families, events, or buildings and homes. The equipment you have when you first start out will greatly influence your income.

*To make more money you can add additional services, such as creating memory movies out of the photos you take. See Memory Movie business idea in this chapter.

Education/Skills:

Knowledge of the use of a variety of cameras, lighting, flash, and how to accurately take a picture is necessary. If you will also be developing the film, you should know how to set up and use a dark room.

Show Me the Money: $$$$

Professional photographers can make a good living by providing school photos, senior portraits, or family photography. You can charge by the hour, $35 to $50, and from $15 to $400 for packages. The annual income ranges from $40,000 to $100,000.

Business Equipment: 📱 ☎ 📄 💿 🖥 🎧 ▭

You should have a top of the line camera, a digital and a 35mm. If you will be providing developmental services, you will need a dark room and dark room equipment. A top of the line photo copier/ printer will also be necessary for the digital camera and to make additional copies of the 35mm photos.

Business Base:

Unless you have a studio in your home a large part of your business will be spent traveling. Around 35 percent of your time will be spent in your home office.

Clientele:

There is no set clientele group for this business.

Starting Point:

You can start by taking nature pictures and selling them as stock photos or sending them to photo contests. You can take photos of friends and families to showcase your talent. You can also establish a Web site where potential clients can view your work.

You can also contact school districts and get an account to take student photos. You may have to offer the school district a percentage of your sales in exchange for using your service.

Learn More:

Online

Training course in photography offered by the New York Institute of Photography is available at **http://www.nyip.com/courses/dp.**

Information on the photography business can be found at **http:// www.homebiztools.com/ideas/photography.htm.**

Books

How to Start a Home-Based Photography Business, 5th (Home-Based Business Series) by Kenn Oberrecht.

Business and Legal Forms for Photographers (with CD-ROM) by Tad Crawford.

How to Open & Operate a Financially Successful Photography Business: With Companion CD-ROM available from Atlantic Publishing.

Professional Fundraiser: ✮ ✮ ✮

Do you like to help nonprofits or individuals who are in need of funds? A professional fundraiser uses the resources of a grant writer and the planning of an event planner to create professional fundraising events in the community.

Business Overview:

Fundraisers obtain the necessary funds for organizations, individuals, and nonprofits in need of capital. Your duties include:

- Planning a community event to raise funds (car washes, benefit dinners, auctions, galas, and so forth)

- Executing the event from start to finish

    o Set up

    o Maintain

    o Cleanup

- Advertising and getting media attention for the event

- Renting space and equipment for the event

- Counting and administering the funds for the organization

The event or type of fundraising will determine other responsibilities and duties.

Education/Skills:

An understanding of fundraising and good time management and organizational skills are musts.

Show Me the Money: $$$

Fundraisers can charge a percentage of the money raised, 10 to 15 percent, per project, between $300 and $2,000, or you can charge a percentage of the total event cost, somewhere between 10 and 20 percent. Professional fundraisers make an annual income of $40,000 to $60,000.

Business Equipment:

You should have, in addition to the basic home office equipment, software for event planning and database software.

Business Base:

This is about 30 percent home-based and 70 percent travel time.

Clientele:

There is no set clientele group for this business.

Starting Point:

Provide your services on contingency for a nonprofit or family in need of funds. There are a number of families whose children need medical attention, but they cannot afford the surgery, medical procedures, or equipment. A fundraising event or benefit dinner can help them raise the much needed money.

Learn More:

Online

Your community fundraising guide at **www.fundraisers.com/ servicesdir/professionalorgs.html**.

Become a fundraising consultant at **www.plannersguide.com/ fundraiser.htm**.

Fundraising professionals go to **http://www.fundraiserpro.com**.

Books

The Accidental Fundraiser: A Step-by-Step Guide to Raising Money for Your Cause by Stephanie Roth, Mimi Ho.

Successful Fundraising: A Complete Handbook for Volunteers and Professionals by Joan Flanagan.

Principles of Professional Fundraising: Useful Foundations for Successful Practice (Jossey Bass Nonprofit & Public Management Series) by Joseph R. Mixer.

Professional Scrapbooker:

Do you enjoy making stories out of photos and designing pages around a certain photo or set of photos? Do you already provide scrapbooks as gifts for family members? If you already enjoy doing this for fun, why not do it for some extra money?

Business Overview: ✯ ✯ ✯

Professional scrapbookers design scrapbooks with family photos their clients provide.

Education/Skills:

A flair for creativity and design are musts.

Show Me the Money: $$

Professional scrapbookers can charge anywhere from $25 to $75 per scrapbook, depending on the number of pictures used, the time, and design equipment needed. The annual income will be in the $30,000 to $50,000 range.

Business Equipment:

Scrapbooks and various scrapbooking equipment, designs, glue, and scissors in a variety of cutting shapes will be helpful. You should be able to find a lot of different ideas and designer items in any craft or scrapbook store.

Business Base:

This is strictly an at-home business.

Clientele:

There is no set group of clientele for this business.

Starting Point:

You should start by providing your services to family and friends. Find a scrapbook store or craft store that you can be affiliated with, giving them your exclusive business in return for informing their customers about your service.

Learn More:

Online

Resources for the scrapbook professional can be seen at **http:// www.scrapbook.com/resources.html.**

The site **http://scrapbooking.com** is packed with information and ideas for scrap booking.

Books

The Scrapbooker's Guide to Business by Kathy Steligo.

Secrets of Scrapbooking Success: Making Money, Making Memories by Sue DiFranco.

The Crafts Business Answer Book & Resource Guide: Answers to Hundreds of Troublesome Questions About Starting, Marketing, and Managing a Homebased Business Efficiently, Legally, and Profitably by Barbara Brabec.

Seamstress: ✮ ✮ ✮

Do you love to sew? Do you have knack for designing or fixing clothes? Why not make a little money while you are providing a service that you enjoy?

Business Overview:

Your main duties include:

- Sewing ripped clothing

- Provide alterations to various clothing garments

You could also design, create, and sell your own personal clothing line, quilts, or blankets for a fraction of the cost of clothing stores. Although if you have a variety of clothes, you might consider a storefront so you can show off your products. If you do have a storefront, you could also sell a variety of sewing and crafting goods for the do-it-yourselfer.

Education/Skills:

Knowledge of sewing and how to use sewing machines, fabric materials, and sewing products is necessary.

Show Me the Money: $$$

Depending on the services you provide you can make anywhere from $20,000 to $40,000 annually. If you own a storefront, you should be able to make $60,000 to $80,000 annually.

Business Equipment:

A sewing machine and a variety of sewing equipment and fabrics will be needed.

Business Base:

This is strictly an at-home business, unless you own a storefront.

Clientele:

There is no set group for this business. Many people do not sew and need alterations.

Starting Point:

Sew clothes and make alterations for family, neighbors, and friends. You can also connect with a clothing store or wedding shop to provide alterations to the clothes that arrive with problems. This partnership could result in contacts for you.

Learn More:

Online

Become a seamstress and pursue your dream as an alteration shop owner at **www.stylecareer.com/alteration_shop.shtml.**

A sewing lesson is the perfect start to becoming a qualified seamstress. Find information at **www.sewinglessons.com/sewinglesson.html.**

Books:

The 'Business' of Sewing: How to Start, Maintain and Achieve Success by Barbara Wright Sykes.

How to Start & Maintain a Profitable Sewing Business: Making Money with Your Sewing Skills by Becky Reed.

Sew to Success: How to Make Money in a Home-Based Sewing Business by Kathleen Spike.

Spa Parties Consultant: ☆ ☆ ☆

Do you enjoy going to parties or being the life of the party? You can create the party while earning money.

Business Overview:

A spa party consultant provides parties at spas. You can provide specific spa party packages and use the following services at your parties:

- Body Wrap
- Gentleman's Facial
- Hot Stone Massage
- Zen Salt Glow
- Spa Facial
- Sugar Body Polish
- Custom European Facial
- Buff-n-Bronze Skin Friendly Tanning

- Pedicure
- Reiki
- Teen Facial
- Toe Glow
- Yoga
- Massage
- Paraffin Foot and Hand Treatments

You could also provide different packages, such as a birthday package and a mother and daughter package. Be creative; think of fun ideas.

Education/Skills:

You need no educational degree to provide these services, but you should have an understanding of massages, as these will be an integral part of your business.

Show Me the Money: $$$$

Spa party consultants can charge anywhere from $20 to $130 (depending on the package, time, and spa supplies needed) per guest with a minimum of 10 to 20 guests. You can make anywhere from $40,000 to $100,000 annually, depending on the number of parties you can handle.

Business Equipment:

You will need a variety of supplies, such as nail polish remover, cotton balls, nail files, orange sticks, nail polishes, scissors, mirrors, bowls, massage oils, wax products, towels, robes, and so on.

Business Base:

This is mainly a traveling business; you might spend a total of 10 to 30 percent of your time in your at-home office.

Clientele:

Women and teenage girls will seek your services. You can also put together business parties and offer business owners a way to thank their employees. Invite them to have a relaxation day once a month or for special occasions throughout the year.

Starting Point:

Provide a party for a neighbor or your daughters, if you have any young girls. Invite all their friends and their parents and provide the party free of charge. You can also put together a free spa party for people in the community who deserve a day off, such as volunteers, veterans, service men and women, teachers, firefighters, police officers, and nonprofit administrators.

Learn More:

Online

Learn the basics of spa parties at **www.partypop.com/Categories/ In_Home_Beauty_Spa_Parties.html.**

Recipes, treatments, and tips for hosting a spa party can be found at **www.arizonaspagirls.com/0/Lifestyle/SpaParties.**

Great spa party ideas and information from moms is available at **http://www.amazingmoms.com/htm/party-spa-party.htm.**

Books

Secrets of the Spas: Pamper and Vitalize Yourself at Home (Life's Little Luxuries) by Catherine Bardey.

The Herbal Home Spa: Naturally Refreshing Wraps, Rubs, Lotions, Masks, Oils, and Scrubs (Herbal Body) by Greta Breedlove.

Girls' Night In: Spa Treatments at Home by Jennifer Worick.

Natural Beauty at Home: More Than 250 Easy to Use Recipes for Body, Bath, and Hair by Janice Cox.

Logo Clothing Design: ★ ★ ★

Create logos for t-shirts, sweaters, sweatshirts, sweat pants, and other team clothing by using silkscreen or embroidery. You can focus on local teams, school shirts, or local business designs.

Business Overview:

Design the logo, create a silk screen of the design, and apply the silkscreen design to the clothes. You can also try to get business accounts and sell concert t-shirts when a certain band comes into the area or design and make shirts for special events in town.

Education/Skills:

Design knowledge and knowledge of creating logos and other business mottos for print and promotional materials will be helpful.

Show Me the Money: $$$

You can make anywhere from $30,000 to $60,000 if you are working with schools and providing local teams with uniforms.

Business Equipment:

You will need a silkscreen machine, paint, large t-shirt irons, iron on equipment, a top of the line printer, an embroidery machine, and various patterns and threading.

Business Base:

This is strictly an at-home business, unless you would like to sell professional sports apparel or something similar. A storefront would be needed if you want to offer a clothing line.

Clientele:

There is no set group of clientele for this profession; your primary patrons will be local event managers, school officials, and coaches.

Starting Point:

Offer a local school a discount on a large order of t-shirts. You can contact local recreation centers about offering your shirts to little league teams. You can also contact other local facilities such as:

- Concert halls
- Universities
- Dance halls
- Cheerleading camps

- Karate or other martial arts
- Rehabilitation centers
- Gymnastics facilities
- Teen centers and after school program directors

Look for local events and design and create t-shirts for those events. You may need a vendor's license to legally sell your t-shirts at local concert halls or other facilities.

This is a relatively new field. There are not many books or Web sites available for this industry.

Videographer: ★ ★ ★

Do you enjoy using the video camera and capturing moments as they happen? Perhaps being behind that camera can make you money.

Business Overview:

Take videos of special events such as weddings, childbirths, birthdays, anniversaries, reunions, and a variety of other special events. Other duties may include:

- Recording videos at special events

- Editing the video

- Adding special effects or music to the video

- Transferring the video to DVD or other formats

You may be asked for additional services.

Education/Skills:

A steady hand and a good eye are most important. However, you may need some knowledge of video editing software.

Show Me the Money: $$$

Videographers often can make about $35 an hour or $250 to $500 per project. The annual income is around $60,000 to $80,000.

Business Equipment:

You should have a camera and recording equipment, as well as a VHS and DVD recorder if your customers want the videos transferred into those formats. Make sure to keep a back-up copy and an extra copy of all the projects you complete. These can serve as examples, but also may come in handy if a family has lost their copy or wants another copy.

Business Base:

This is more of a travel business. Only about 20 percent of your time will be spent at the in-home office.

Clientele:

There is no set clientele group for this profession.

Starting Point:

Film a family member's or friend's wedding or special event or tape a charity event for a nonprofit to get referrals and earn contacts in your community. To add additional money to this business you can have a partner who takes photographs.

Learn More:

Online

Video University at **http://www.videouniversity.com.**

Digital producer resources are available online at **http:// digitalproducer.digitalmedianet.com/**.

Books

Light: Science and Magic: An Introduction to Photographic Lighting by Fil Hunter, Steven Biver, Paul Fuqua.

Cinematography: Image Making for Cinematographers, Directors, and Videographers by Blain Brown.

Notes of a Retired Wedding Videographer: From Proposal to Reception; Lessons Learned from Brides and Grooms by C. F. A. Weiss.

Wedding Planner: ✭ ✭ ✭

A wedding planner is very similar to an event planner. The only major difference is that wedding planners focus on weddings, rather than a variety of events.

Business Overview:

A wedding planner consults with the soon-to-be bride and groom and essentially takes care of all aspects of the wedding, from ordering flowers to selecting a venue and ensuring everything runs smoothly.

Education/Skills:

No particular knowledge is necessary, but having a strict attention to detail and excellent management skills would be helpful.

Show Me the Money: $$$

You can charge 10 to 15 percent of the total expenses, a per project fee of $300 to $1,200, or an hourly rate of $25 to $70. Depending on your clientele you could make anywhere from $40,000 to $80,000 annually.

Business Equipment:

You will need a good planner or planning software. Database software could be used to organize contacts, along with pricing and information about their services.

Business Base:

This is a traveling business for the most part. You might spend about 30 to 40 percent of your time in your home office making phone calls and scheduling the event.

Clientele:

Brides, grooms, or parents of the couple will seek your services.

Starting Point:

Contact local banquet halls, country clubs, or other halls of interest. Give them information about your business and see if you can have an affiliate relationship with one of them. Consider having an affiliation with a DJ, a caterer, a party rental place, a bakery specializing in wedding cakes, a balloon company, a florist, and any other wedding associated business.

Learn More:

Online

Guide to becoming a wedding planner, with wedding planning resources can be seen at **http://www.topweddingsites.com/ become-a-wedding-planner.html.**

Become a certified wedding planner at **http://www.aa-wp.com/.**

The Association of Certified Professional Wedding Consultants is at **http://www.acpwc.com/weddingconsultant.shtml.**

Books

How to Open & Operate a Financially Successful Wedding Consultant & Planning Business: With Companion CD from Atlantic Publishing.

FabJob Guide to Become a Wedding Planner by Catherine Goulet, Jan Riddell.

Start Your Own Wedding Consultant Business: Your Step-By-Step Guide to Success by Eileen Figure Sandlin.

SUCCESS STORY: THE PRESS GANG

Skip Press started his business, The Press Gang, in 1996 after holding an active, working journalist position.

"I started it because the opportunity arose once I wrote a certain book. Plus, my kids were small and someone had to look after them during the day. It was easier for me to do it since I didn't have a "steady" job," Press said.

He formed the business over 11 years ago, and it has grown into a monumental success with thousands of students and clients seeking his expertise. Read more about Skip Press here. You also can visit him at **www.skippress.com.**

His business	I'm a writing and screenwriting teacher, author, editor, screenwriter, and consultant.
How his idea was sparked	I was asked to write a book called The Writer's Guide to Hollywood Producers, Directors, and Screenwriters' Agents.
Why he started his business	So I could be a "Mr. Mom" while my kids were growing up.
The pros and cons	Pro – I make my own schedule and meet many new friends. Con – I don't know where my money is coming from, month-to-month.

SUCCESS STORY: THE PRESS GANG

Type of business	Sole proprietor - Home business
His main concern in his first few years of business	I didn't know if people thought I was qualified enough to advise them. I overcame that when the praise became rather constant.
He saw a steady flow of income in...	It was immediate and has remained so.
His likes and dislikes about running a business	I like helping people get closer to their dreams. I dislike it when I can only take them so far and they don't quite reach their goals, which isn't really my fault because I do my best and other clients make it.
Future aspirations for his business	Becoming much better known as an author and probably making my own movies.
His qualities that help in his business	I know what I'm talking about and I don't fake it when I don't.
The key to his success	I genuinely care about others.
A challenge he faced while running his business	When asked to write *The Complete Idiot's Guide to Screenwriting* I didn't know if I was qualified. So I sat down and studied other available books and saw that most of the authors were not as qualified as myself, and that there were a great many things missing from the other advice books. So I knew I could make a great contribution. The Writers Guild of Canada said mine is the best available screenwriting advice book.
Advice to potential owners	Know your stuff.
The ease of breaking into his industry	Hollywood is a very tough business to break into, unless you're a cat burglar. Writing overall, however, is much easier, particularly in the area of non-fiction.

SUCCESS STORY: THE PRESS GANG

His business day	Vacations disrupt my business because I'm the only one doing the business. I'm usually involved in some aspect of my work 16 hours a day, 6 days week, except for time for meals and errands.
What he believes it takes to be successful in business	You have to love writing and editing and people.
When he knew his business was a success	One of my writing class students got a three-book deal.
His most bizarre request	That I write a screenplay based on someone's idea – no fee – and that we split the proceeds 50/50. Of course, he didn't become a client.
His most embarrassing moment	A lunatic client reported me to the Better Business Bureau when I didn't like his very bad screenplay. The BBB didn't give his complaint credence when they examined the facts.

Chapter 5

Profitable Businesses For Students

"If your success is not on your own terms, if it looks good to the world but does not feel good in your heart, it is not success at all."

-Anna Quindlen

The following information is set up a bit different from the previous chapters, but the importance and profitability of these businesses are still the same. These businesses are good ways to offset or provide an additional income to other businesses we have previously covered.

Although they can be started as primary businesses, you may want to add them to an already established business or a business you might be interested in starting. We have provided these business's sister business; if you review them, you will gain the information needed to begin these businesses as additional services or as its own business.

Expense Reduction Specialist:

Reduce the expenses of small businesses and corporate spending. Help business owners find solutions to bringing more money in and less money going out.

Sister Business

Business Consultant – Chapter 3

Resources

Articles and resources on reducing your business expenses through Microsoft can be found at **www.microsoft.com/ smallbusiness/resources/articles.mspx.**

Collection Agent:

Help businesses obtain the funds and money that their clients did not pay for.

Sister Business

Medical Billing Coordinator — Chapter 3

Resources

Biz resources for collection agencies at **www.biz-resources.com/ collection-agencies.htm.**

Computer Programmer:

Help businesses write programs to aid in their business's success in a variety of formats.

Sister Business

Computer Repair Specialist — Chapter 4

Resources

Computer programmer's careers can be found at **www. careeroverview.com/computer-programming-careers.html.**

Estate Sale Specialist:

Estate sales take place everyday. Whether the owners are deceased or the family plans on relocating to another state, there is a growing need for someone to run the sale.

Sister Business

Rental Agent – Chapter 3

Resources

Planning an Estate Tag Sale info at **http://reviews.ebay.com/ Planning-an-Estate-Tag-Sale_W0QQugidZ10000000000033792.**

Go Antiques can be seen at **http://www.goantiques.com/ community/resources/estate_sales.htm.**

Campaign Manager:

Run campaigns for nonprofits and political leaders in your area.

Sister Business

Personal Assistant — Chapter 3

Resources

The Campaign Manager: Running and Winning Local Elections by Catherine M. Shaw, Michael E. Holstein.

Notary Public:

Hundreds of documents need to be witnessed and signed in front of a registered notary public. You can do this with no education and as an addition to many businesses.

Sister Businesses

Bookkeeper — Chapter 3

Accounting Services — Chapter 3

Business Consultant — Chapter 3

Resources

Become a notary through the national notary association at http://www.nationalnotary.org/howto/.

Laundry Service Specialist:

Provide laundry-cleaning services by picking up and dropping off clothes for those who do not have a washer and dryer at home

Sister Business

Seamstress — Chapter 3

Pet Groomer:

Pet groomers make an animal look like a king by bathing them, clipping their nails, and cutting their hair.

Sister Businesses

Animal Breeder — Chapter 4

Animal trainer — Chapter 4

Resources

Articles and resources for pet grooming are available at **http://www.propetgroomer.com/**.

Operating a pet grooming business information can be found at **http://www.groomingbusinessinabox.com**.

Pet grooming products are available at **http://mjmcompany.com/ pet-grooming-products.htm.**

Restaurant Delivery Service:

Many high-class restaurants do not offer delivery services, but if you have a reliable vehicle and a hot bag, you can offer the service for the restaurants. They take and make the order and you pick it up and deliver it.

Sister Businesses

Personal Chef — Chapter 4

Cake Decorator — Chapter 3

Word Processor/Typist:

If you simply want to type or you want an addition to your business, typing can be the key. Many writers or editors write with pen and paper and that is where you come in.

Sister Businesses

Virtual Secretary — Chapter 3

Desktop Publishing — Chapter 4

Resources

Typing positions for home typists can be found at **http://www. typeinternational.com.**

Western Publication Association at **http://www.wpa-online.org.**

Editor:

Editors make sure all written work is proofread and free from editorial errors. You can use any of the freelance links provided at the beginning of Chapter 3 to find jobs you can bid on now.

Sister Business

Freelance Writer — Chapter 3

Resources

Editorial Writers Guild at **www.edsguild.org**.

Consultants:

Do you enjoy giving one-on-one instruction? Consultants are merely experts in the field they provide consultant services in. There are a number of consulting businesses that you can start. The following links will give you an understanding of the business you choose.

Fashion Consultant:

StyleCareer.com provides insider tips for fashion and image careers **www.stylecareer.com/stylist.shtml**.

Careers in women's fashion consulting site offers fashion news, features, and columns, shopping, designer galleries, as well as a fashion database all at **www.fashion102.com/fashion6/careers-in-womens-fashion-consultant.html**.

Image Consultant:

America's Image Consultant Institute at **www.aici.org**.

ImageMaker, Inc. is your premier source for training on becoming an image consultant at **www.imagemaker1.com**.

Links to resources and training for becoming an image consultant can be found at **http://www.fashionforrealwomen.com/Image_Consultant_Training.html**

Legal Nurse Consultant:

American Association of Legal Nurse Consultants at **www.aalnc. org.**

Get the hands-on experience you need to be a successful legal nurse consultant at **www.rnmarket.com.**

Legal nurse consultant schools and nurse paralegal programs at **www.legalnursingconsultant.org.**

Computer Consultant

The Independent Computer Consultants Association (ICCA) at **www.icca.org.**

NACCB is an association of computer consultant businesses dedicated to promoting the industry and business success — **www. naccb.org.**

Aimed at computer consultants for small businesses. Offers small business support and software packages at **www.smallbiztech talk.com.**

Financial Consultant

An international association for registered financial planners at **www.iarfc.org.**

How to Become A Successful Financial Consultant by Jim H. Ainsworth.

Court Advocate:

A court advocate is the liaison for the courtroom and the victim. He or she works for the victim and is paid by the courts to make sure the victim is strong enough to testify and has the moral support needed to get through the court experience.

Sister Business

Life Coach — Chapter 3

Resources

Every state and county has specific resources. You can go through your state's Web site to view specialized information locally.

Training for advocates available at **http://www.apowerfulvoice. org/training.htm.**

National Court Appointed Court Advocates at **http://www. nationalcasa.org.**

Court Runner:

When lawyers do not have the time to go back and forth to the courts for simple paperwork and various other reasons, a court runner makes the time and earns a decent living doing so.

Sister Business

Personal Assistant or Virtual Secretary — Chapter 3

Mediator:

A mediator is the calm, reasonable voice between two people going through divorce, child custody cases, and business partnerships. Mediators make their living finding solutions to life's domestic and business problems.

Sister Business

Life Coach or Inspirational Speaker — Chapter 3

Resources

Resources for mediators can be found at **http://www.**

directionservice.org/cadre/indexformediators.cfm and at http://
www.keybridge.org/resources_mediators.htm.

Travel Agent:

Travel agents help their clients plan the perfect vacation. They find
and arrange all airfare and sometimes accommodations for their
clients.

Sister Business

Vacation Rental Agent or Rental Agent — Chapter 3

Resources

Home-based travel agent resources are available at **www.home-
basedtravelagent.com/resources.htm**.

Travel agent resources directory can be found at **www.
travelworldnews.com/agent**.

Travel agent resources at **www.travelagentresourcecenter.com**
and at **www.travelagentacademy.com**.

Costume Designer:

Design and create Halloween or school mascot costumes. Whether
you plan on selling nationally or online, this can be a rewarding
and lucrative business or business addition.

Sister Business

Seamstress — Chapter 4

Resources

Costume resources at **www.costumepage.org/tcpmake2.html**.

Coolest ideas and tips for making Halloween costumes can be found at www.coolest-homemade-costumes.com/making-halloween-costumes.html.

Fashion CAD pattern making software for making costumes at www.cadcam.solutionsaustralia.com.au/Costumes.htm.

Database Specialist:

Businesses need databases created and maintained for a number of reasons: client contacts, employee contacts, business expenses, and a variety of other business needs. This can be a fun and challenging business or business addition.

Sister Businesses

Administrative Assistant — Chapter 3

Virtual Secretary — Chapter 3

Resources

Very Large Database at http://www.vldb.org.

Database resources at http://www.freeprogrammingresources.com/database.html.

Career Coach:

Make a career out of helping others find a career. Whether you are working with handicap individuals and showing them the ropes of their new career or helping people find the perfect career for their personality, you will enjoy the flexibility.

Sister Businesses

Inspirational Speaker — Chapter 3

Life Coach — Chapter 3

Career Coach Institute: **www.careercoachinstitute.com**

Elder Supervisor:

Senior citizens that live alone and in nursing homes need an extra eye and someone to help them with daily care and appointments.

Sister Business

Hired Companion — Chapter 3

Resources

Resources for senior care at **http://www.resource4seniors.com/** and **http://www.seniorresourcesec.org/**.

Staffing Service:

Helping businesses find the right employees can help you earn a living.

Sister Business

Business Consultant — Chapter 3

Resources

Staffing services resources at **http://www.insourcesolutions.com/resources.asp.**

SUCCESS STORY: LAW OFFICE OF WILLIAM J. AGNEW, JR.

Actually, a good friend of mine (another lawyer) and I got this crazy idea to start writing screenplays and that is the new venture I would like to start." Read how his adventure began and how he makes it on his own.

His business	I represent people who have been accused of violating the laws of the State of Texas. My wife is my office manager/receptionist/secretary/paralegal.
How his idea was sparked	A more experienced lawyer kept telling me I could make a much better living as a criminal defense lawyer because I liked to try cases.
Why he started his own business	It was really the next logical step for a criminal prosecutor in a small town such as Lufkin. There was nowhere for me to move up as a prosecutor. I had gone as far as I could go as a prosecutor in East Texas.
The pros and cons	PRO: I answer to myself, so I have complete freedom. I love that aspect of this. If I want to cut out early to ride my bicycle or play golf, there is no one to say no. Also, I am an insulin dependant diabetic, and the freedom from running my office from my house makes it much easier to remain compliant with my diabetic requirements. I can test my blood sugars and take my insulin when needed without any additional hassles or preparations. It allows my diabetes to be an extremely minor inconvenience. CON: I do not have a steady source of income I can depend on. When I am not working, I do not get paid. When times are slow, you begin to wonder if you are ever going to make any money again.
Business Type	Sole proprietor - Home business
His most bizarre request	A client's mother asked if I would pay for her father's funeral.
His main concern in his first few years of business	My two main concerns were cash flow and adequate representation of my clients. I overcame them by working hard and taking cases for less than other lawyers. As for the adequate representation, I had an older lawyer who guided me through the steps necessary to transition from prosecutor to criminal defense lawyer. His office supplied me the proper knowledge, forms, and paperwork needed to run my own law office.

SUCCESS STORY: LAW OFFICE OF WILLIAM J. AGNEW, JR.

Saw a steady flow of income	Believe it or not, by the end of my first year I had almost doubled my previous government salary.
His likes and dislikes about running a business	I love the lack of structure. I am a free-spirited person, and I love being able to call all the shots and do things how I want. I don't have to follow anyone else's rules. Dislike: Criminal defendants and their families can be very demanding, especially when they are in jail awaiting resolution of their case. It gets frustrating when they are constantly demanding things that are not reasonable or having to bear the brunt of their frustrations for a situation I did not put them in.
Challenge faced	We don't have a steady flow of income. I hold out a set percentage of every dollar I make and put it in a savings account to help compensate for the slow times.
Future aspirations for his business	Given the approach I have taken to practicing law, I can turn away clients I do not feel comfortable representing because I do not have tremendous overhead. I do not have the pressure of having to take cases solely for the money. I just hope things continue the way they have been the last few years. I am fortunate in that I can be a lawyer first, businessman second. I enjoy being a lawyer much more than a businessman. If things maintain they way they are right now for the next 20 to 30 years, with adjustments obviously for inflation and cost of living, I will consider myself a very lucky person.
Qualities that have helped	My ability to take a risk and not be afraid of a new challenge.
The key to his success	I hope it is my trial skills, which I'm proud of. In all honesty, I think it is that I conduct myself with honesty and integrity. Whether it be prosecutors, judges, or clients, I feel people know I am not going to lie to get a better deal, or to win at trial, or to get someone's money.
His advice to potential business owners	Keep it simple. Too many people go all out at the beginning and get over-extended on their expenses. The less you have to pay out each month, the more you get to keep of what you make. Gross income looks nice, but net income is what you get. I focus on the net, after expenses. I try not to incur more debts than I have to.

SUCCESS STORY: LAW OFFICE OF WILLIAM J. AGNEW, JR.

The ease of breaking into his industry	Depends on where you live. Right now, in Texas, I think it is not easy to break into. We have too many lawyers in Texas, and we keep churning more out twice a year.
His business day	I work around 40 to 50 hours a week, depending on the week. We do take vacation days; however, since my wife is the only other person in the office, it disrupts our business a lot when we vacation. With cell phones, call forwarding, and the Internet, we are able to compensate somewhat. However, nothing ruins a vacation more than working during it. With each step we take to not disrupt the business, we disrupt the vacation.
What he believes it takes to be successful in business	You need to be self-motivated and willing to do the work without someone telling you what to do. I think it also helps to treat people the way you want to be treated. The worst thing I see other lawyers do is treat other lawyers, clients, or judges in a disrespectful manner. Your reputation as a person can do wonders for you, or make your job much more difficult. As the old saying goes, you catch more bees with honey than with vinegar. I think that particularly applies to the legal profession.
When he knew his business was a success	I was in Wal-Mart with my soon-to-be wife, and I realized how much money I had made that month and I had quite a bit more coming in. It was much more than I had dreamed of making at that point in my life. I realized I no longer had to shop at Wal-mart. I have hardly been there since.
His most embarrassing moment	My mother, who had been recently released from a mental hospital, came to stay with me for a couple of months. She was a chain smoker and would sit outside talking to all my clients when they would come to meet with me. She would listen to their stories and believe every word of whatever they said and then come tell me how they were all innocent. They all liked her, but it made my job a hell of a lot more difficult. "Your mom thinks I'm innocent, why don't you?"

Chapter 6

The Business Plan

"The majority of men meet with failure because of their lack of persistence in creating new plans to take the place of those which fail."

-Napoleon Hill

Business plans are the most essential part of getting your business off the ground and in finding funding for your business. A business plan simply has the essential information about your business, such as who the key players are and a summary of your business, including the products and services you will be using.

Consider hiring a business plan writer if you feel you do not have the necessary writing skills. A professional business plan writer can research and write your plan as in-depth or basic as you would like it to be written. The research that is involved in writing about your finances, market analysis, and competition can become very time consuming. Hiring a business plan writer can greatly eliminate the errors or other misinformation in your business plan. But their fees can range anywhere from $5,000 to $15,000, which is determined by the size or difficulty of your plan and the research needed.

To save money you can write the plan yourself. In this section we will show you how. And if you get writer's block or you would like a second opinion log onto **www.score.com** and find a local SCORE office near you, where you can take your plan and discuss it with others.

The Importance of Custom Business Plans

Your business plan should include the following:

- Executive summary
- Mission statement
- Business structure
- Management team
- History and position to date
- Supporting documents

- Products and services
- Business strategy
- Financial plan
- Summary
- Industry Overview/ Market Analysis

Each of these sections will be broken down in the next section so you can better understand and more easily beginning writing.

While you are writing your business plan, ask yourself, "Why should this investor bring his millions to me?" Make sure you answer that question in your plan. You want investors to see your business's potential.

Step-by-Step Guide to Business Plan Writing

Throughout the business plan, we will use the fictitious company, American Windows, as an example. American Windows is a company that has been in business since 2004. Its only employee, John Michaels, wishes to expand. He is producing a business plan to expand his services and to seek funding through financial companies.

The following examples are only short examples designed to

give you an idea of what should be included in each section. The sections of your business plan should be much more in-depth and contain more information about your company, your plan, and the people in your business.

Executive Summary

The executive summary will be the first thing potential investors see, so make this section stand out.

The executive summary states what the purpose of your business is. It offers potential financiers an overall view of your business and the types of services/products you will be producing. The more detailed it is, the better, but try not to add anything irrelevant, like cutesy anecdotes.

Your executive summary should summarize the following questions:

1. What is the purpose of your company?

2. What is the current status of your company?

3. What are the products or service you are offering?

4. Who is your target market?

5. What are your company objectives?

6. What are your financial plans?

Let us look at American Windows's executive summary.

AMERICAN WINDOWS EXECUTIVE SUMMARY

American Windows is a window sales and service company located in the Seattle business district. It began in 2004 in the home of John Michaels, who has worked in the window industry for the past 13 years.

AMERICAN WINDOWS EXECUTIVE SUMMARY

Mr. Michaels is currently the company's chief owner and advisor. American Windows is a sole proprietorship. Since its debut American Windows has increased its customer base and is looking to expand in the area and offer a faster turn-around time for its current and future clients. Upon its expansion American Windows wishes to offer industrial and commercial windows to its clients. With the word of mouth advertisement the company has received in the past six months, it cannot handle the load of orders it currently has.

An expansion to a large warehouse where the windows could be produced quickly and efficiently would place further emphasis on customer satisfaction. Mr. Michaels also wishes to hire three employees to help handle the orders and to help produce the windows.

Over the next few years, profits are expected to grow from $100,000 to $500,000. Mr. Michaels is looking to receive a loan of $90,000 and a line of credit of $82,000 to buy additional molding equipment and hire sales staff, window staff, and administrative staff during the following two years.

History and Position to Date

The history and position to date section asks for the step-by-step startup of your business. It should answer the following questions:

1. What is the company's background?

2. Why will your business succeed?

3. If you have numbers through market research that indicate the need for your business, insert it in this section.

4. Do you have any sales from previous years? If so, write them in this section.

5. Does your company have any achievements or special publicity?

American Windows's history and position to date example:

AMERICAN WINDOWS HISTORY & POSITION TO DATE

Windows are an important aspect to any home; they keep the weather out and let the sunshine in. The window making industry has thrived in every city across the world; everyone needs a home and every home needs a window. American Windows plans to continue to grow and capitalize on that industry with a focus on storm-proof windows and customer satisfaction.

Currently there are no storm-proof windows on the market. These windows will fill a void in the market and provide important features, such as shatterproof glass, see-through insect screens, and an automatic steel garner.

American Widows has won the national award for great new home invention at the house and home show in downtown Seattle for three years straight. The company has also increased its sales from a mere $5,000 a year to $100,000, last year's sales figure. With our achievements and happy clients we are ready to offer our windows to a larger demographic and introduce them into the commercial fields.

Your Mission Statement

A mission statement is one short paragraph indicating the plan and purpose for your company. Your mission statement will be used for a number of purposes, including the incorporation documents. You should also have the mission statement somewhere on your Web site.

An example of a mission statement for American Windows is

AMERICAN WINDOWS MISSION STATEMENT

To provide quality windows at an affordable price to the community through tireless research, up-to-date industry training, and certified employees. To be the leading manufacturer of home widows with an emphasis on safety, energy efficiency, and individual customer satisfaction.

They are very simple to write and draw mostly on why your company exists, whom you plan to serve, and what your main goal is for the future.

For help with writing this section log onto:

http://www.bplans.com/dp/missionstatement.cfm

http://www.homebiztools.com/mission.htm

http://www.resume-resource.com/coverwriting.html

Business Structure:

For this section, you need to answer the following questions:

1. What is the business structure and which state is it under?

2. For what reason did you structure the business this way?

Here is what American Windows might write for its business structure:

AMERICAN WINDOWS MISSION STATEMENT

American Windows is a sole proprietorship under the state of Washington. The structure will help ensure the ownership of Mr. Michaels and his sole control of the growth and expansion of the company, products, and services.

Management

When you are putting together the section on management and you are the only employee, you will only have to answer a few questions about yourself:

1. What is your experience?

2. What is your title?

3. What are your skills and industry knowledge?

You will have to write about yourself in the third person, like the following example:

AMERICAN WINDOWS MANAGEMENT SECTION

John Michaels, CEO of American Windows, started the company in the summer of 2004 after working in the window manufacturing business for 11 years. His creative and innovative ideas for new window designs helped create the bay window and other significant designs that are used in homes all across the world.

Products and Services

This section will emphasize your current products and services and potential products and services. Any and all products and services should be listed here to show all potential investors what you will be concentrating on in your industry. Here is what American Windows might say:

AMERICAN WINDOWS PRODUCTS & SERVICES

American Windows will offer quality windows at competitive rates, thus giving the client more for their money. With the sole location of the office in Mr. Michaels's basement these goals have been reached without renting office space or the renting of various other inventory spaces. American Windows has received over $100,000 in net earnings. With new clients and a waiting list of commercial buildings that would like to use the services of American Windows a factory is needed. There are a variety of window styles to accommodate any home and business, including the newly designed storm-proof window, which is made with steel garners to withstand hurricane force winds.

On top of the high-quality windows the company produces, American Windows also offers installation services to the client, thus providing everything the client might need for the perfect window.

AMERICAN WINDOWS PRODUCTS & SERVICES

American Windows plans to develop a number of new window designs to make the modern home more manageable, with cost effective products and energy efficient window seals.

Industry Overview/Market Analysis

This section includes an industry overview of the other major players or competition in the area and industry. It does not matter if the majority of your business is online, at-home, or in a storefront; there will be competition. This section is where you summarize the competition and emphasize why you are different. Let us take a look at the industry overview for American Windows:

AMERICAN WINDOWS COMPETITION

The current competition includes two local window companies:

1) Tempro Windows is an exclusive home window installation business that has been in the Seattle area for the past 10 years. Tempro Windows employs 30 individuals for the sale and installation of the windows with an annual net worth of $500,000.

2) Merchant Windows is an exclusive construction factory creating windows for business and large structures. Merchant Windows has been in business for 5 years and has had sales soar into the millions in the last two years. They employ hundreds of window installers for commercial businesses. Both these competitors have a weak pricing and sales force, which has pushed potential customers to purchase windows from factories and install them personally. When installation is not done accurately weather leaks increase the amount of energy the consumer uses, which will be a marketing strategy for us. American Windows plans to offer commercial and home windows with a rate much lower than both of these companies and a quality above industry standard.

For additional help with market analysis Entrepreneur Magazine offers samples of analysis and planning forms for your business.

They offer a variety of analysis forms, including competitive, demographics, market planning, cost analysis, location selections, and market research methods. Visit them at **http://www.entrepreneurmag.com.**

Business Strategy and Implementation

Your business strategy and implementation section will focus on your business's approach, such as how you plan to execute your daily business, new services you plan to promote, new products you are planning, and any marketing techniques you plan to implement to find clients.

American Windows might write a business strategy like the one that follows:

AMERICAN WINDOWS BUSINESS STRATEGY

American Windows plans to increase the consumers' understanding of energy efficient windows and proper installation with a promotional mail awareness campaign. The company will use brochures mailed to residences and businesses in the area to inform them of:

1. Our new expansion and service of commercial buildings.

2. Proper window installation and the savings this could ultimately put back in their pockets.

3. Our pricing and custom design windows, to save them money and increase the value in their homes.

With the increase in sales from our word of mouth advertising we plan to increase our sales staff, training them to keep our customer satisfaction a priority, and offer significant rebates to our past customers for bringing in their friends and family.

We plan to attend and have a small vending table at all house and home shows in the area and to offer a savings package for customers at that time.

For help with business strategies Entrepreneur Magazine offers samples of business strategies and planning forms for your business. Visit **http://www.entrepreneurmag.com.**

Financial Plan

For this section you will have to answer questions about financial matters, such as your current annual net income and your advertising budget. This section is a thorough breakdown of all the money coming into the business and going out of the business, such as:

- Salaries
- Storefront rent
- Promotion
- Office supplies

- Insurance
- Inventory
- Maintenance
- Sales

Any other expenses you can think of, as well as startup expenses, will need to be added. Let us look at what American Windows might write for this section:

AMERICAN WINDOWS STARTUP EXPENSES
American Windows currently has an annual net income of $75,000. With the purchase of a downtown warehouse for $250,000 and an additional sales staff, which will cost $60,000 annually, we will be able to triple the amount of customers we can handle and offer our services to commercial buildings, which will bring in an additional $1,000,000 annually.

You should also include a table or chart such as the one below:

SERVICES/PRODUCTS	REVENUE
Product/service 1	
Product/service 2	
Product/service 3	

Miscellaneous Products and services	
Total Revenues	

EXPENSES	DIRECT COSTS
Materials	
Equipment	
Salary	
Wages	
Miscellaneous Expenses	
Total Direct Costs	

For additional help with financial planning log onto **http://www. entrepreneurmag.com**. Entrepreneur Magazine offers samples of financial planning forms for your business.

Summary

These are the last words your potential lender will read; make them memorable. This section should also provide a summary of your entire business plan in a concise manner. Be sure to sound confident about your business's future in this section. Here is how American Windows would summarize their plan:

AMERICAN WINDOWS SUMMARY
American Windows plans to be a significant part of the Seattle window sales industry, due to our current plans to show the community the amount of money they can save in the purchase and installation of windows, along with the energy savings over an extended period of time.

Supporting Documents

Any supporting documents that you have, such as potential clients, financing documents, past client referrals, letters of recommendation, and/or any other supportive documents that might give a more in-depth overview of your company, should be submitted along with your business plan.

Presenting Your Business Plan

When you have completed your business plan, you should consider the presentation of your plan. You should contact your local office store and ask about spiral binding, with a clear front cover and a solid cover for the back. Do not staple your business plan or bind it with leather.

Resources for Senior Entrepreneurs

The site, **www.bplan.com**, offers sample business plans for a variety of businesses, along with advice on writing your business plan and links for other sources.

Entrepreneur Magazine is dedicated to the start-up of home-based businesses. Visit them at **http://www.entrepreneurmag.com**.

Office Depot (**www.officedepot.com**) offers free forms to download for small businesses.

SUCCESS STORY: ART TECHNO MARKETING	
Nora Boyle started her business in 1990. She worked a lot of low-end publishing jobs, as a 'clerk jerk' in broadcasting and for magazines, but none of these jobs would lead her to either higher salaries or any opportunities for advancement.	
Her business	I work as a consultant on contract as a technical writer, editor, Web developer and designer, and in marketing.

SUCCESS STORY: ART TECHNO MARKETING	
How her idea was sparked	I met consultants doing similar work or who asked me to help them.
Why she started her own business	To stay employed and to choose the sort of work I enjoy.
The pros and cons	I work on contract and if you manage it correctly, you can take time off and name your price.
Type of business	Sole proprietor - Home business
Her main concern in her first few years of business	It is a continuing struggle to find work, but the biggest obstacles are commuting if you can't work at home, Also, choices of software and problems with licensing and upgrades, both at home and for clients, and matching expectations.
She saw a steady flow of income in...	I made money as soon as I went on my own.
Her likes and dislikes	There is no security and no benefits.
Future aspirations for her business	I like to write fiction and want to write and sell that.
Personal qualities that have helped	Leadership and a can-do attitude always help.
The key to her success	A standalone spirit or independent thinking.
A challenge she faced while running her business	Often, you find you cannot meet the expectations of other people, and you have to cut your losses and move on. People skills are the most difficult, especially in the creative realm, so you learn to reserve judgment, practice diplomacy, and realize you cannot control the universe, though you will run into people who truly believe THEY can.

SUCCESS STORY: ART TECHNO MARKETING	
Her advice to potential business owners	First, talk to people who are doing the sort of things that interest you and see what steps they took to get there. You have to develop a seeking spirit or you will never cross the many rivers that it takes to get ahead with your skills and talents, and then you have sell them. It is important to always learn how to sell, because everything is selling.
The ease of breaking into her industry	No, it's not easy. Originally I wanted to write for TV, and although I possessed the talent and drive, I really didn't get to the jobs I wanted. So I learned to write for TV anyway and use those skills in other areas, such as computer graphics, commercial advertising, and in scripts I write for fun. There is a saying, "this leads everywhere…" and it means that you cannot narrowly define your goals or dreams, or you will never enjoy the journey of getting there.
Her business day	40 hours a week plus weekends. I've taken months off and traveled around the U.S.
What she believes it takes to be successful in business	A strong desire is the bottom line, but keeping pace with technology, current events, and being adaptable to people and places and cultural differences is also important.
When she knew her business was a success	People from all over the country contacted me.
Her most bizarre request	Someone asked me to baby-sit their cats.
Her support group	There are many support groups, but I only belong to one or two and join in on the occasional blog.

Chapter 7

Establish Your Business

After you have decided on the business you would like to create and have proven to yourself, through the self-evaluation chapter, that running a business will be the best move for you and your family, let us take some time to learn how to make your business a legal entity. The following section on establishing your business provides a step-by-step guide to starting your business and filing all your business forms from start to finish.

Select a Business Name

When you are trying to decide on a business name, think of something that will stick in people's minds when they first hear it or say it. Your business name should identify who you are and what you are selling or the service you are providing. It has to be a name that has commercial and industry appeal. **Let us look at a few examples:**

- Memories in Motion – What does it make you think about?

- Jiffy Lube – Do you know exactly what service they provide?

- Circuit City – Do you know what kind of business that is?

- Sexy Nails – Do you know what you are going to get?

Obtaining an Employer Identification Number

An employer identification number, or EIN, is your business's social security number. In fact, if you are a sole proprietor, you can simply use your social security number instead of applying for an EIN, unless you plan to hire employees some time down the line; then it is recommended you apply for one. It is easy to obtain, but it is important, as it is used on every form and business filing. This will be one of the first things you will apply for and should be done right after you choose your business name.

Business Entity Search

When you find a perfect name for your business the next step will be to search through your state's home page to be sure the name is not being used by another company. The list below provides, by state, a link to where you can search for a business name. This only applies to the state you are conducting business in; you can still use a name that is in use in another state.

STATE LISTINGS	
Alabama	http://www.alabama.gov/portal/secondary.jsp?page=Business_StartingaBusiness
Alaska	www.state.ak.us/local/businessHome.html
Arizona	http://az.gov/webapp/portal/topic.jsp?id=1158
Arkansas	http://www.state.ar.us/business_res.php
California	http://www.calbusiness.ca.gov
Colorado	http://www.colorado.gov/colorado-doing-business/
Connecticut	http://www.ct.gov
Delaware	http://delaware.gov/egov/portal.nsf/portal/Business
Florida	http://www.myflorida.com/taxonomy/business/
Georgia	http://www.georgia.gov

STATE LISTINGS	
Hawaii	http://pahoehoe.ehawaii.gov
Idaho	http://business.idaho.gov
Illinois	http://www.illinois.gov/
Indiana	http://www.state.in.us/information_business.htm
Iowa	http://www.iowa.gov/state/main/business.html
Kansas	http://www.kansad.gov/business/
Kentucky	http://kentucky.gov/Portal/Category/BUSINESS
Louisiana	http://www.state.la.us
Maine	http://www.maine.gov/portal/business
Maryland	http://www.dat.state.md.us/sdatweb/checklist.html
Massachusetts	http://mass.gov
Michigan	http://www.michigan.gov
Minnesota	http://www.state.mn.us
Mississippi	http://www.state.ms.us/index.jsp
Missouri	http://www.business.mo.gov/
Montana	http://mt.gov/business.asp
Nebraska	http://www.nebraska.gov
Nevada	http://sos.state.nv.us/business/
New Hampshire	http://www.nh.gov/business/index.html
New Jersey	http://www.state.nj.us/njbusiness
New Mexico	http://www.newmexico.gov/business.php
New York	http://www.nysegov.com
North Carolina	http://www.ncgov.com/
North Dakota	http://www.nd.gov/category.htm?id=69
Ohio	http://business.ohio.gov/
Oklahoma	http://www.ok.gov/1350/
Oregon	http://www.oregon.gov/menutopic/business/bus_dev_starting.shtml
Pennsylvania	http://www.state.pa.us/papower/taxonomy/taxonomy.asp?DLN=29888
Rhode Island	http://www.ri.gov/business/

STATE LISTINGS	
South Carolina	http://www.sc.gov/Portal/Category/BUSINESS_TOP
South Dakota	http://www.state.sd.us/
Tennessee	http://www.tennesseeanytime.org/business/index.html
Texas	http://www.business.texasonline.com
Utah	http://business.utah.gov/business/starting.html
Vermont	http://vermont.gov/doing_business/start_business.html
Virginia	http://www.virginia.gov/cmsportal2/business_4096/index.html
Washington	http://access.wa.gov/business/start.aspx
West Virginia	http://www.wv.gov/sec.aspx?pgID=3
Wisconsin	http://www.wisconsin.gov/state/core/business.html
Wyoming	http://wyoming.gov/business.asp

Select Your Business Structure

It is important to research the best way to structure your business. The structure should accommodate the type of business or service that you will be offering to the public. Provided in this section are the business structures you can file.

Sole Proprietor

The sole proprietorship is the easiest, quickest, cheapest, and least complicated business structure to create and file for. The sole proprietorship essentially means that you and your business are one. It is the same for tax purposes with a sole proprietorship—you and your business are one. Therefore, the income of your sole proprietorship is taxed to you, as opposed to the business otherwise structured. Another potential benefit of having a sole proprietorship is the tax benefits you can receive. You have the ability to take a portion of your earnings and place them in an investment account without having to pay taxes on them; this plan is called the Keogh Plan.

General Partnership

There are two types of partnerships you can apply for; a general partnership is the most common. The best way to start your partnership is to create a partnership agreement, which illustrates the responsibilities of each partner, the earnings, and how they are divided. In a general partnership both partners' personal assets are at risk. One partner can sign any documents or legal actions regarding the business without the other partner knowing, which will ultimately legally bind both partners. Yet, each partner should agree to work with the other in good faith, loyalty, and fairness. General partnerships offer the same retirement plans as sole proprietorships. In terms of income tax, the partnership does not pay taxes; instead they file a return telling the IRS how much money the partnership earned or lost, and then the partners pay taxes on his or her share of income.

Limited Partnership

A limited liability partnership combines the best aspects of the general partnership and the corporation. The major difference between the general partnership and the limited partnership is that the limited partner is not personally liable for the business's debts. A limited partner is merely an inactive partner in the business; perhaps he offers the capital, while the other partner manages the business structure. He or she can only lose the capital he paid or agreed to pay or has received from the company after it became insolvent. The limited partner cannot be active in the management of the partnership. The limited partnership can be as costly and as complicated as a corporation.

Special Corporation

There are two forms of specialty corporations, outside the regular corporation (C corporation) and an S corporation. These include the professional corporations and nonprofit corporations.

The professional corporations, referred to as professional corporations or professional service corporations, include professionals who wish to incorporate their services, including:

- Healthcare industries
- Engineers
- Lawyers
- Social workers
- Veterinarians
- Accountants

Every state varies on the regulations for filing for a professional service corporation. Contact your state to see if your services can be considered for this type of corporation. The rule of thumb is, if you are organized for the sole purpose of providing professional services, you would most likely file for this corporation.

The nonprofit corporation is formed if you are considering having a 501 (c) 3 status, which allows your corporation to be exempt from IRS taxes. The legal reason for forming a nonprofit corporation is for the purpose of religion, charity, literacy, science, and/or educational purposes. The basic rule of thumb is that you are not in it for the money, but for the purpose. Nonprofits rely heavily on grants and governmental funding to provide their services, while many of the services they provide to the public are free or for a small fee. A partial list of purpose groups that should consider filling a 501 (c) 3 are:

- Churches
- Performing arts schools
- Libraries
- Political Groups
- Health clinics
- Child-care centers

- **Homeless shelters**   • **Museums**

There are a number of rules that govern the responsibilities of running a nonprofit organization. You should check with your state to see if the service you are performing could be considered for 501 (c) 3 status; however, it can be complicated and time consuming to file for this status.

Limited Liability Company

A limited liability company is one of the newest corporate structures and is gaining in popularity. The members of an LLC enjoy limited liabilities on their personal debts. Although many state laws governing the LLC are still developing, it is a favorable structure for many small businesses. Many states require that there be at least two members, but that can be solved if you have a spouse who can be named as the other member. The LLC can choose to either have pass-through taxes or be taxed as a regular entity. The normal procedure for taxing an LLC is through the pass-through tax, which means the taxes for the business pass-through to the individuals, just a sole proprietorship is conducted. You and the company are one, and you pay the taxes as one. But you can elect to be taxed like a corporation, where the company will be taxed for its earnings, and then you are taxed for your individual earnings.

"S" Corporation

The "S" corporation allows corporations to be treated like partnerships. The corporation does not pay taxes on the company but instead passes the income on to their shareholders who then pay taxes on that income through their income tax rates, thus allowing shareholders to take business losses on their personal income tax returns. To be eligible for S corporation status you have to be consistent with the following rules:

- Your company is a U.S. company with no more then 75 shareholders (husband and wife counts as one).

- Shareholders are individual U.S. citizens or resident aliens.

- The corporation only has one form of stock (for example: one voting and the other non–voting).

- The corporation does not own more than 80 percent of stocks in another company.

- All shareholders must sign an "S" corporation status form and file it with the IRS.

"C" Corporation

When you incorporate your business you will first be considered as an "S" corporation. You must take an extra step to become a "C' corporation, called an election. The majority of small-incorporated businesses are privately owned. The corporate stock is often owned by one person or a few people, and the shareholders are actively involved with the day-to-day operations. The most identifiable feature of a regular corporation (or C corporation) is the fact that the business is an entirely different entity than the business owner. Incorporation is the most costly way of doing business, as you not only have to pay a hefty incorporation fee, you also have to pay annual fees to your state. There are many regulations and procedures to running a business, and all shareholders must be a part of the decision-making process. But incorporation limits your liability to law suits. If you had no intention of defrauding creditors, your home and personal bank accounts and other valuable property cannot be touched. C corporations are treated as a tax-paying entity that is separate from its investors and must pay corporate federal income tax. Before you decide on incorporation take an in-depth look at doing business as a sole proprietor, partnership, or LLC.

Family Businesses

Many small businesses are formed so the whole family can be a part of it. The children can one day run the business and families can learn, bond, and grow together. There are a few special rules and tax breaks for family-owned businesses. Some benefits include:

- Family businesses allow for income splitting. This is a technique in which the higher bracket taxpayer (the mother or father of the business) shifts the income to the lower paying tax bracket (like the child or grandparent).

- You can pay high wages to your spouse and children as long as they do real work and the pay is reasonable.

- You can transfer a family-owned business to a younger generation family member to reduce estate tax liability after death.

If family members will be shareholders, you will have to file for a partnership, an LLC, or incorporate for the IRS to consider this as a family business.

Business Licenses

Almost every business needs a permit or license to conduct business, no matter what type of business you will run. There are normally licenses that are needed at all levels of the government. Most are very simple to apply for, but to legally do business in your state, city, and county you will need to make sure the type of business or service you are providing does not or does need one to conduct your business. Let us look at those levels a little closer.

Federal

The federal government does not ask that small businesses get a license or permit to run their operations unless they produce any one of the following products or services:

- Investment advisors

- Ground transportation (busses or trucking companies)

- The preparation of meat products

- Production of drugs

- Production of alcohol, tobacco, or the dealings of firearms

State

You will have to search through your state's business Web portal, listed above by state, to see if the service or products you are producing need to have a license. All states differ, but if you are rendering any type of professional service, you will more than likely need a license to practice in your state.

City and County

There could be a number of licenses and permits needed on the local level. The following local departments can assist you in obtaining the correct permits or licenses:

- City or county clerk (ask about regulations for the type of business you are running)

- Building and safety department

- Health department (if your business uses food handling or preparation of any kind)

- Zoning department (to get permits to remodel a storefront or obtain information about your home-based business: be sure your neighborhood is zoned for an at-home business)

- Your local IRS or tax office

SUCCESS STORY: KOLA'S KORNER.

NeKola Permenter started her home-based business, Kola's Korner, in January of 2004. "I still work a regular job while running my business. You have to until your income from your business equals/exceeds what you make during a month from your regular job. I can't wait for the day I don't have to work another job," said NeKola.

"I was a legal secretary before I started my business. I started this business for health reasons (stress on the job) and because I wanted to spend more time with my daughter," NeKola continued. Her Maryland-based business can be found on the World Wide Web at **www.kolaskorner.com**. Read more about NeKola's ambitions and her story here and be sure to visit her on the Web.

Her business	Your one-stop gift shop. Simplifying your shopping experience by offering shopping for any occasion — all from one location.
How her idea was sparked	Just talking with a group of women. I wanted to give people one place to shop for great gifts at affordable prices.
She started her own business	I started my business for my daughter and for health reasons (stress on the job is not worth the money).
The pros and cons	PRO: You have more time to spend with your family. CON: Not having enough money to place ads, participate in events, and the like.
Business Type	Sole proprietor — home business
In her first few years of business	Building a customer base (without customers you can't make money). Talk to everybody you know (don't be shy about it –I'm still working on that). Be patient. Find a good support group.
Saw a steady income flow...	Two years and still going.
Her likes and dislikes about running a business	Like: Receiving a call from a customer telling me how happy they are with the product. Dislike: When items are backordered (loyal customers you keep, new customers you can lose).

Success Story: Kola's Korner.	
Qualities that have helped	Being a people person.
Future aspirations for her business	I want the future to be a prosperous.
The key to her success	Advertising (FREE and paid), word of mouth, and good customer service.
Challenge faced while running her business	Family not being supportive. I did a lot of research and joined some online groups. I made a lot of new friends that way.
Advice to new owners	Don't ever give up, no matter how hard it gets.
Her Business Day	It depends. Some weeks I work more than others, but on average 20 to 30 hours. I am able to take vacation whenever I want.
Ease of breaking into her industry	Yes and no. It all depends on what your product is.
Potential earning in her industry	Having a unique affordable product is key.
She believes it takes to be successful in business...	Know your product(s) and get to know your customers. If you don't know the answer, tell your customer that you will get back to them in the next 24 hours with the answer.
Her support group	My daughter and other entrepreneurs are my biggest supporters.
Knew business was a success when	I made $1,000 for two hours of work.
Most embarrassing moment	Calling a customer by the wrong name. Thank goodness she understood and still shops with me.

Chapter 8

Establish A Home Office

If you have a separate room in your home that can be converted into a home office, that would be a good place to create an office. Having such a space will make starting your business that much easier. However, not everyone has a spare room, and your office might need to be in a family room, den, living room, or even in your room. This is especially true for students who may be living in a dorm or some other type of community living. To adequately pick a location ask yourself these simple questions:

- Does this area offer enough space for a desk, equipment, and inventory (if needed)?

- Are electrical, cable, and Internet outlets available?

- Do you have proper lighting?

- Is there enough space for you to conduct large projects (if needed)?

- Can the noise be controlled from this area?

- Is the room sufficient to your comfort level?

Creating a Home Office

If you are setting up a spare room office, it is imperative that your family, friends, and classmates that may visit know the rules and expectations you have. Therefore one of the first things you need to do is write a set of rules for the home office.

You can create a sign...

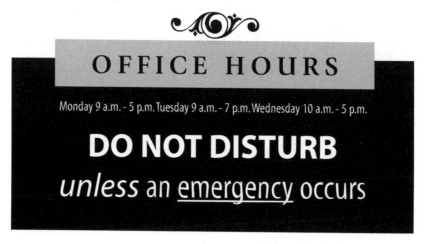

OFFICE HOURS

Monday 9 a.m. - 5 p.m. Tuesday 9 a.m. - 7 p.m. Wednesday 10 a.m. - 5 p.m.

DO NOT DISTURB
unless an <u>emergency</u> occurs

Or you can post written rules and place them on the door of your dorm room or home office. For example:

- When this door is closed DO NOT DISTURB.

- When the door is closed and it is an emergency, please tell me.

- This is not a playground; no toys allowed.

- No drinks permitted EVER.

These are just a few examples of some of the things you can do for your rules.

Beyond the signs you should also be sure to sit down with your family or roommates, let them know even though you are at home that does not mean you are not working. Tell them to pretend you are at a regular office.

Equipment

The majority of businesses need a home computer, printer/fax machine, landline, and possibly a cell phone. Take a moment to check off all the things you currently have to start your business. Then you can take your list to the store and have an outline of everything else you will need. Some of this you may need to go without if you are in a small dorm.

OFFICE EQUIPMENT CHECKLIST		
☐ Desk	☐	Cell Phone
☐ Computer	☐	Comfortable Chair
☐ Printer/Fax Machine	☐	Storage Shelves/Closet/
☐ Separate Phone &	☐	File Cabinet
Business Phone Number	☐	Business Cards
INITIAL OFFICE INVENTORY CHECKLIST		
☐ Printing paper – both white and designer		
☐ Large calendar		
☐ Software (depending on your business)		
☐ Pens, pencils, and writing utensils		
☐ Small office supplies (tacks, white out, stapler, etc).		
☐ Blank CDs & DVDs		
☐ Business Cards		
☐ The Products You Sell		
☐ The Products Needed to Create the Products You Sell		

Leasing a Storefront

If you plan to lease a storefront, there are a number of other steps that you will need to take. Before you decide on the location of your storefront make sure you address the following questions with the building owner or landlord:

- What is the crime rate in the area?

- Is the building maintained well?

o You should get a feel for the building when on a tour.

- What other types of businesses are in the area?

    o You do not want to be too close to competitors.

    o It is nice to be close to businesses that are an off-set of yours; for example, say you run a specialty paper store, being next to an ink store would draw customers to yours.

- Does the store have adequate lighting?

    o Inside and outside the building.

- Is it large enough for your business?

    o Be sure to include room for inventory and for the space to greet and/or meet your clients.

- Is the building insured?

    o Be sure they have personal injury insurance, in case a customer falls in the front of your store.

- Does the rent exceed your potential monthly earnings?

- How long does he need the lease to be signed?

- Is the neighboring community in good shape?

- What are the buying habits of the neighboring community?

- Do they show pride in their community?

    o If you are in a neighborhood that takes pride in their community, they are more inclined to buy from a neighborhood mom-and-pop store.

You may have more questions. Write them down as you think about them and discuss them with the landlord.

Getting Your Storefront Up and Running

After you have decided on the storefront to rent, it is time to get it up and running. Let us start with the design and theme. You should pick a theme that is associated with your business in some way or one that fits the clientele you are trying to attract. For example: If your target market is senior citizens you are not going to want your theme to be zoo animals. You want your target market to feel comfortable in your store.

While you are designing, it would be a good idea to also implement a floor plan, including where you will place racks, if you are selling clothes, and where to put display cases and other items that need to be scattered throughout the store. Be sure to have enough room for your customers to walk through the store.

If you are finding it hard to understand your target market, ask someone from your target market what type of theme they would like.

When you have chosen a design and a theme, it is time to put it all together and think about a creative way you can incorporate your theme into a grand opening celebration. For example: Say your target market is toddlers, and your theme is zoo animals. Have door prizes, as well as gifts to the first 1,000 customers. You could give away stuffed animals or sippy cups with animals on them as door prizes. For more details about a grand opening, see Chapter 9.

The next step to setting up your office, after the design of the building, is to complete an inventory of items you are selling. Use the floor plan you have already designed to help you navigate.

Set up all utilities for the building; most will already have the electricity and water on, but you will need to have the phone (with voicemail), Internet, and any other necessary utilities connected.

Organization

Everything you sell, every contact you make, and every idea you have should be written down and organized in a file cabinet or other document safety box.

Below is a list of items that might help you stay organized:

- Storage bins and a storage bin utility shelf

- Name tag creator (name bins by content for easy access)

- Storage drawers

- Desktop organizer (for pens, paper clips, and push pins in)

- A large dry erase board and/or corkboard (with a calendar or without)

- You can have weekly inventory checklists printed up at a local Kinko's or office store

Being organized also means keeping a consistent schedule. Whether you are using a home office or a storefront you should have and stay on a schedule. Make certain, though, if you are the only one running the storefront/home office, that you close the doors at least once a week and close at a decent hour throughout the week. Giving yourself down time will be a much-needed commodity once you get the business going.

Write down the schedule you would like to keep, and then go over this schedule with your family or roommates. Will this schedule complement everyone else's schedule or will there be conflicts? If so adjust accordingly and make the necessary changes to ensure a smooth transition

Financial Record Keeping

Get at least one software program for keeping your financial records. Software program options include: Intuit Quicken – **www.quicken.com** and Microsoft Money – **http://www.microsoft.com**. You may be lucky enough to use the computers at the library if they have these programs. If you do, then use a memory stick and back up your records on it each time you visit. You may also be able to make use of other school provided items. See what all your tuition covers and what amenities you can use during your enrollment. You could get printing privileges that could save you money. You might be surprised at what all you can make use of.

There also are a number of financial record books you can buy from local office supply stores. These books have spaces designed for keeping your financial records and information and helpful tips on keeping this information together.

SUCCESS STORY: REGINA SOKAS, LCPC	
Regina Sokas worked for others as a therapist for 15 years, but wanted to start her own practice in the mental health industry. "I wanted to be able to practice the way I want with fewer constraints and more independence," Mrs. Sokas said.	
In September of 2007 Mrs. Sokas created Regina Sokas, LCPC in Maryland.	
Her business	A sole practitioner, private practice offering individual and family therapy.
How her idea was sparked	Worked in the field for 15 years and wanted the independence
Why she started his own business	To be able to practice the way I want with fewer constraints.
The pros and cons	Pro — Very interesting work Con — State licensure requires advanced degree and years of supervised practice. Some liability risk.

Success Story: Regina Sokas, LCPC

Type of business	Sole proprietor – Office space
	I looked at LLC when my brother, a psychiatrist, was going to join me, but that fell through.
Her main concern in the first few years of business	Still in the first year. Major concerns were/are: 1) Getting referrals in the door. 2) Learning how to manage the financial end, as before I worked for someone else and only had to do the therapy. I did not have to worry about billing insurance companies, just collected a salary.
She saw a steady flow of income in…	Business tends to be seasonal, with summer very slow. So I'm starting to get a slowdown. I would say that it took five months to see any real money coming in and it is slowing now. I still have to figure out the cycle a little better – how much do I need during busy months to float the slow ones because steady is not an option.
Likes and dislikes	I love meeting people and giving real help to them. I dislike trying to get paid sometimes.
Qualities that have helped her in her business endeavors	I'm flexible. So if Plan A didn't work, I could come up with a Plan B, C, or D. I don't scare too easily. And I believe very firmly in my ability to learn new things.
Future aspirations for her business	This is never going to be a nationwide franchise or a get-rich scheme. But I anticipate being well known in the community, having a steady income, fewer unfortunate "surprises" in my bookkeeping, and continued feelings of freedom and pride.
The key to her success	Persistence. Some things take multiple trials.

SUCCESS STORY: REGINA SOKAS, LCPC

A challenge she faced while running her business	The public medical assistance program is often complex and rigid, which may be why very few private practitioners will see these clients. However, as these people are often in the most need of help, I was determined to persist. Success has only been the result of regular phone calls to find out what I did wrong this time and continue to refine my paperwork. It wasn't exciting. It wasn't pretty. But it's working now (most of the time).
Her Business Day	At 35 I'm not killing myself, but if you don't work, you don't make money.
Her advice to potential business owners	Make sure you have enough money set aside so that you can weather the lean times in startup. Anticipate that the big agencies will take three times as long to process your documents, as you'd like, so start early and follow up often.
The ease of breaking into her industry	Requires education and training, but after that, yes.
The potential earning in her industry	Probably not what most people think of as "good income." You may clear $50,000 a year.
What it takes to be successful in business...	Learn to market. Learn the financial end. Do good work so referrals will come in.
Her support group	I have some friends and family that have been supportive.
When she knew her business was a success	I'm still insecure enough that I'm not 100% sure.
Her most embarrassing moment	I'm in the mental health business, but have not had anything really bizarre. We may have a different tolerance for bizarre.

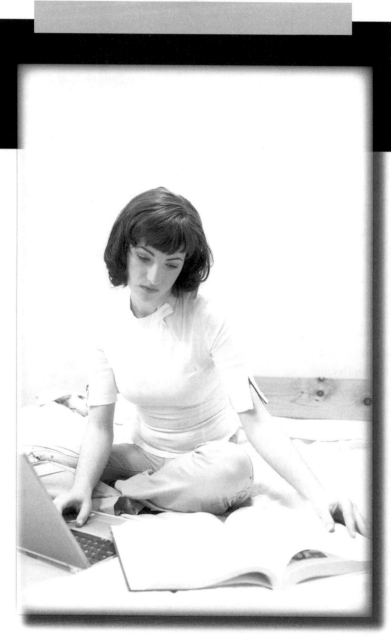

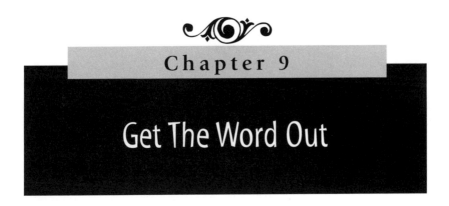

Chapter 9

Get The Word Out

Advertising

Advertising is your company's only means of letting your potential customers know you are there. You need to use some form of advertisement, and doing so is a major necessity. You will use advertisement throughout the course of your business, and you will need it when you:

- Add a new product or service.
- Hire a new employee.
- Change current products/ services.
- Want to coordinate a contest.
- Change hours of operation.
- Do humanitarian work.

These are just a few great opportunities to use advertising. The rule of thumb is if anything significant changes in your company, use advertising to let the public know. You can offer the advertisement in a variety of forms:

- A press release.

- Ad in community papers.

- Put flyers up in community centers, restaurants, department stores, or clinics your clients might use.

- If this is for school age children, contact a school principal in your area to see if you can give them enough flyers to hand out to each child in school.

Word of mouth is one of the best advertising venues available today, and the best thing about this form of advertising is that it is free. Word of mouth advertising requires a lot of energy, as well as patience, politeness (even in the face of rudeness), and a fresh attitude with every customer.

Venues of Advertisement

There are a number of different ways to reach your target market; some may cost more than your budget allows, while others may be free. The following are venues of advertisement:

- Local small press/ School Papers
- Major newspapers
- Local television networks
- Flyers/Brochures
- National television networks
- Local business commerce booklet
- Phone book
- Direct mail
- Radio stations
- Web site
- Local events
- Host a charity drive

Local Small Press Papers

Local small press papers often are found at any area bank, grocery store, department store, or other shopping centers. They are always free and offer local news and entertainment. Most of these small presses will allow you to place a free ad of 25 words or less. In major cities you may find three or four of these small presses. You can also try your school paper. It may be very inexpensive to run your ad with them and you would help them by purchasing the ad.

Major Newspapers

Every city has its own major newspaper; some larger cities have more than one. The major newspapers are normally published daily, with a larger volume produced on Sunday. Newspaper ads will work best if your marketing objectives include targeting a specific region or neighborhood. Advertisement rates can get expensive, but you will gain the needed exposure.

The cost of your advertisement depends on the day it will be advertised and the amount of space you would like to purchase. There are a number of choices when purchasing your ad. You can choose:

- Full page
- ½ page
- ¼ page
- 2″ column
- 2 ½″ column
- 1″ column
- 1 ½″ column

You can offer small coupons in the paper or a free service or product to first time clients. This will bring the customers in and, if your service or product is exceptional, create your word of mouth advertisement.

To be sure your advertisement will be read by those consistent with your target market ask yourself or the newspaper's advertising sales staff a few short questions:

1. Will the location on the page make a difference?

2. Who are the general readers of the paper?

3. Which day of the week should my ad run?

4. What section of the paper would work best for the product/ service I am providing?

You also might want to contact other papers, especially if you can sell your product/service on a national level. For a list of newspapers locally and around the globe check out **www.newslink.org**. You will find every paper (small and large) in print today locally and nationally.

Questions:

Consider asking if the newspaper has a section for new businesses. Many papers offer this as noteworthy or newsworthy information, and you can get spots for free.

Press releases are also placed in the newspaper free of charge. A press release is a one-page article detailing what is happening with your business. Here is a sample press release that I wrote for a client:

SAMPLE PRESS RELEASE

FOR IMMEDIATE RELEASE:

LEARN HOW TO WRITE FOR THE MOVIES FROM SCREENWRITING VETERAN SKIP PRESS

Are you a movie fanatic? Have you ever thought of better ways to have movies end, characters react, or had the image of an entire movie in your head? Have you ever watched a movie and thought, "Hey, I could have written that!"

If you answered yes to any of the above questions, there is no better time to enroll in Skip Press's instructional screenwriting course, "Your Screenwriting Career." A two-decade veteran of Hollywood, Skip Press teaches the necessary formula to make any writer's celluloid dreams come true. He has written professionally for radio, TV, video, and film and achieved honors like the Silver Medal at the New York International Film Festival.

Press has shared his Hollywood knowledge and experience through three editions of his Writer's Guide to Hollywood Producers, Directors, and Screenwriter's Agents and two editions of *The Complete Idiot's Guide to Screenwriting* (and a Russian version). His most recent tome is *The Ultimate Writer's Guide to Hollywood* from Barnes & Noble Books.

SAMPLE PRESS RELEASE

Now, in your local university or community college you can take a course so popular it is being offered in well over 1,000 colleges around the world and to the U.S. military. "Your Screenwriting Career" is offered at these local universities and community colleges:

In six weeks, you will learn how to turn your idea into a completed screenplay. The course includes instruction on the history of storytelling, building strong characters, creating memorable dialogue, and crafting powerful storylines. Correct format, rewriting, and marketing are all covered. See **http://www.screenwritingcourse.com** for details.

While there, browse the reviews from former students. Here is one example:

"I thought this was a wonderfully useful and complete introduction to screenwriting. It was encouraging and realistic, and Skip Press did an excellent job of answering questions promptly and fully. I would recommend this course highly to anyone interested in the subject area."

Who knows? You could be the next successful screenwriter walking out of the movie theater yelling, "Hey, I wrote that!"

###

Media Contact:
Heather Shepherd
419-340-2432
writing4peace@msn.com

Local Radio Stations

Radio advertisement can be expensive, but if your advertisement runs at the right time and on the right stations it can be a big boost for your product/service, especially if one of the more popular DJs is the one advertising your product.

You will want to be sure your advertisement is broadcast on a radio station that your target market is listening to. But how do you know what kind of music your customer listens to?

1) What is the age group of your target market?

2) What are the demographics of your target market? Do they live in the city, suburbs, on campus?

3) What are the major radio stations in your area?

Then you can either contact your local radio stations to find out what their target audience is or listen to the stations. When you figure out which station has the same market as you, you know where to advertise. Contact the station about pricing, the best rating times, and how much an ad during that time will cost. You want to be sure your target audience is listening when your ad runs.

Local TV Networks

Advertising on local TV networks can be much more expensive than radio advertising and can cost upward of a few millions dollars, depending on when your ad runs. In addition, you will have to pay for the production of the commercial, which can cost about the same amount as the run rate.

National Television Networks

Advertising rates for national television networks can be even higher than your local networks. In addition to the costly run of your ad on television, you will have to pay for the production of the commercial, which can cost about the same amount as the run rate for the national television networks.

Phone Book

As soon as you get your company off the ground, contact the local phone book right away. They publish the phone book yearly, but stop accepting names for the next year just three-quarters of the way through the year, usually sometime after September.

Phone book ads are billed on a monthly basis so be sure to include that in your budget. It is suggested that you place something small at first, including your business name, short motto, phone number, and address.

Direct Mail

We covered the basics of direct mail in the first chapter. You can use the same type of correspondents as you did for the direct mail questionnaire; however, your postcard might look a little different. An example of what a postcard might look like is above.

Flyers/Brochures

You can design a flyer or brochure using a number of different computer programs. You can place them at local retailers and offices or you can post them around the city. You can also use them in a direct mailing campaign.

Web Site

No matter what type of business you are running a Web site is a must. This format offers almost unlimited advertising possibilities.

If you have no HTML experience and do not have any idea about creating a Web site, many Web hosting companies can help you.

There are a few options you can explore:

- Use your Web host's design program. Most Web hosting companies have design programs that can be edited online. These programs are often user friendly and make it easy to design a beautiful Web site.

- You can hire a Web designer. If you are not tech savvy in any way, you can have your Web hosting company make you one. They will also provide the management of the site.

- If you know a little HTML and you have a Web design program, you can download themes or templates. I designed my Web site (**www.heathershepherd.com**) with a theme by Round the Bend Wizards.

Web costing companies range in fees by the month and the year. I use **GoDaddy.com** and pay a mere $40 a year.

Local Business Commerce Booklet

Every area has a local chamber of commerce, which produces a booklet that offers advice and business listings. Being a part of the chamber can greatly boost your company's image. Many local businesses only work with other chamber members. They do charge a member fee, but the benefits greatly outweigh the fees.

Local Events

Local events can be an excellent way to inform the public you are open for business and willing to help the community. There are a number of ways to provide support and earn leads and new clients while you do it, including:

- Sponsoring a little league team.

- Sponsoring charity events.

- Providing coupons or donating items for benefit events and charity events.

- Volunteering at various events in the community.

- Provide gift certificates to outstanding students and/or humanitarians.

- Sponsor or help with various nonprofit organizations.

- Keep up to date with house and home shows (if your product or service is associated with this industry) or with annual wedding seminars.

Being involved in some sort of humanitarian effort is a way to get free publicity for your company. Let us say, for example, that your grandfather, father, or brother was in any one of the wars, and every month you offer a free product/service to those in the armed forces. This would be a great story the news media would want to cover.

Those are just a few ways that you can slant your humanitarian story. If you do have a humanitarian effort and a good back story to go with it, think about creating a publicity campaign.

Create a Publicity Campaign

Let us pretend that you had a failed high school education and you want to promote Read for Literacy, a nonprofit organization that helps children and adults learn how to read. Your efforts to help could start with a press release title like, "Before I owned my business I couldn't read." Adjust the content to emphasize your struggle in school and as an adult. Now you and your company are trying to prevent others from enduring that struggle.

For the next year every form of media contact will revolve around that simple theme, "Learn to read." Every promotional item, every ad campaign, every press release will mention your effort to help someone read.

Host a Charity Drive

You can host a charity drive in your community. To start you will need to first decide on the theme of your drive. Let us say, for example, you own a seamstress business. You could sponsor a coat drive for kids. The coats have been used and may require sewing.

Therefore, you offer your services to sew up any holes in the coats, which will then be donated to children. Get the radio stations involved and have local businesses sponsor the event. You can get local restaurants or stores to donate gift certificates for prizes or have a raffle throughout the day where the proceeds go to a children's charity, a food bank, or some other nonprofit organization.

Plan Your Grand Opening

When you are ready to open your doors for service you should have a grand opening. If you have a stay at-home business and own a Web presence, you should plan on having your grand opening on the Web or do it during a trade show or other community event.

If you are merely having a grand opening on the Web you can send out a press release to local papers informing them of your grand opening and what specials you have. When you do a Web-based grand opening extend the event throughout the first month you are open, instead of a week or day as storefronts do.

If you own a storefront make it a major party that will last a day or a week. Offer door prizes, gifts, or gift baskets with your product to the first 1,000 customers, Have a drawing for a big prize and have fun introducing your product or service.

One great place to shop for gifts and other small items to offer as prizes for the drawing or as door prizes is **www.orientaltrading. com**. You can also visit other party stores in your area, which could spark a great idea for your grand opening.

Protecting Your Trademarks or Intellectual Property

Protecting your trademarks or intellectual property for businesses, such as freelance writing, is important. You can view information and download the appropriate forms at the U.S. Copyright Office at **www.copyright.gov**. It is easy to obtain copyright and only costs around $25 per piece. Trademarks, on the other hand, can cost as much as $125. For other questions regarding trademarks or copyrights log onto the U.S. Copyright Office's Web site.

SUCCESS STORY: STREET CORNER PRESS, INC.

Scott Stewart started his writing and editing business in Nevada and Minnesota. "I was a network engineer, which included lots of computer and Web work, tech writing, and so on, and I felt it was turning into a dead-end job," he says. "I wanted to have my young children grow up seeing that you can pursue your dreams and make them a reality."

In 2000 Mr. Stewart created Street Corner Press, Inc. and has been running the business ever since. You can read more about his business here and online at **www.streetcornerpress.com** and **www.abcwriter.com**.

His business	My services include copywriting (commercial and technical), editing, ghostwriting, teaching classes and seminars. I also serve as a writing coach and provide research and publishing guidance. Actually I market and work with clients across the country, thanks to the Internet. I started the business in Nevada but currently live in Minnesota.

SUCCESS STORY: STREET CORNER PRESS, INC.	
How his idea was sparked	Desired to write full time, but knew I had to have concrete projects and not just write for creative reasons on speculation. That's where the copywriting came in and I became an independent pen for hire.
Why he started his own business	Independence and pursuing my desire to write in a true occupational sense.
The pros and cons	PRO: Setting your own work schedule so you can increase family time. CON: No regular paycheck and no benefits like subsidized health insurance and so on.
Type of business	Originally sole proprietor then incorporated. At home. I had a studio/office, but I still did most of the writing at home and most meetings were on-site for clients, so the commute time and rent detracted more than added.
His main concern in his first few years of business	Finding clients and generating more income. Networking through professionals. Introducing myself to businesses. You have to pound the pavement. Pursuing projects that were longer term with phased payment schedules.
He saw a steady flow of income in…	Ha… Still working on that one. (Actually started overlapping projects within 18 months.)
Potential earnings	Are excellent. But you have to work, study/research, and network to get there.
Likes and dislikes	Love getting paid for doing something I like to do. Freedom to live in different areas. Dislike the paperwork, licenses, and everything you need to conform to government regulations.
Future aspirations for his business	I've contracted to go on a national tour to teach business writing seminars. Three books coming out in the next year as personal projects instead of work for hire.
Qualities that have helped in his business endeavors	Personable. Passion. Listening to others/clients and zeroing in on their wants and needs. Brainstorming to find new approaches to find or expand writing projects.

SUCCESS STORY: STREET CORNER PRESS, INC.	
The key to his success	God. You have many highs and lows when you're trying to create your own business. Keeping this response simple; I've seen too many, what you could call, "answers to prayers" to ignore this.
His support group	Yes. Family and friend support is extremely important. Prayer is, too. You not only need to have faith in yourself and those close to you, you need to know they have faith in you.
A challenge he faced while running his business	I was working on a writing project and e-mailing each section as it was done over a two-week period. About a week after the final section was sent, the company called to ask where the material was. I replied I had been sending it to them in sections over that two-week schedule. I never received any server reject messages, but I said I would transmit them again. It was sounding like the old "check's in the mail" line, but I sent them again. The next day they called and asked when I was going to send the sections. I said I had and reconfirmed the e-mail address. This is when I asked about follow-up messages I had also sent without attachments. They checked the e-mail box and said there was no sign of them either. This was a bit puzzling; then I asked if they were running spam filters. They were. They took a look and found all my e-mail had been directed into their dump folder that, fortunately, had not been emptied the last month. They had the material and I didn't look like someone giving them a line of nonsense. This proves phone follow-up is a good thing.
Workday challenges	Regaining lost time. When you're working from home, others think you're free to do other things or visit. Making sure family and health are taken care of. Unexpected expenses that can creep up on you.
His advice to potential business owners	Keep the structure simple, test the waters, and pursue it part time first if you still have another job. Build your contacts and business. Be aware of the extra time and costs you are accountable for as your own employer and not having job benefits. Have some kind of savings

SUCCESS STORY: STREET CORNER PRESS, INC.

	or money you can access to reduce the stress of how you're going to pay your necessities. In the best picture, you should have enough funds to carry you at least six months if not for a year. I know most people don't have that... I didn't, but I did have a retirement fund I could withdraw from early and my wife also had her job. The point is: Try to slide from your current work into the work you want and be prepared for major shifts in your personal economy.
The ease of breaking into his industry	Most people are encouraging and there are always some who will find it to their benefit to also help you out. It can be fairly easy to break into; it's making a living at it that's difficult.
His business day	45 to 60 hours on full workweeks. This helps allow and make up for other time used for family, trips, events, and so on. I'd like to keep weekends free, but often will have a work spillover.
What he believes it takes to be successful in business	Perseverance. Hunger for learning and reading. Willing to listen and work with other people (even though this is supposed to be your "own/independent" business). Learn to schedule and budget. Network with people in a variety of industries... you never know who needs a writer's help.
When he knew his business was a success	Projects started overlapping and opportunities were being provided from clients of clients. You want to grow/have several rings/tiers of references and customers.
His most bizarre request	A client who wanted to publish, as he put it, "white trailer trash recollections, recipes, and cartoons" and to have it marketed exclusively through a major store chain.

Chapter 10

Financing Your Business

One of the major questions you and other entrepreneurs like you are asking is, "What do investors look for?" The answer to that question is simple: a good idea and an individual who can exploit that idea well.

An investor's decision relies heavily on the execution of your business plan; if your business plan is not written well or put together well, an investor will close the door on your idea. Even if you have a well thought out plan and have prepared it satisfactorily, the number of plans that make it to final approval are very low. For the thousands of business plans that are placed on investors' desks only about 500 business plans are examined carefully. Of those 500 plans only around 25 are pursued to the negotiation stage and from there only about six or so are actually invested in.

Investors want to know that your product or service is in demand or is currently being used. You should test your business out without putting any money out or before you begin starting your business. Doing so will show potential investors how your product was used, considered, and how much the clients enjoyed it. Be sure to get a short questionnaire to the clients and get pictures, or evidence, of your product or service's effect on the client or business. Apply all this information to your business plan to help potential investors make a more positive decision about investing in you and your product.

When you do contact investors make sure the following questions can be answered:

- What type of money do you need?
- How much money to you need? What will that money be used for specifically? Such as:
  o $2,000 for a computer system
  o $10,000 for employee startup
  o $600 for a digital camera
  o   Make each money need as detailed as possible to give the investor a complete picture of your needs.
- When will you need the money?
- What are you offering your investors in return?
- When will the money be paid back to your investors? What type of return will be given?
- What exit routes are offered to the investors?

Exit routes are a way the investors can pull their money out if needed or if the company crumbles before its time. Exit routes include share repurchase and private sale.

Forms of Financing

There are a few forms of financing that can help your company get off the ground faster and give you a better chance of succeeding.

Startup Loans

Startup loans are no different than regular loans where you get the money with the intention of paying back the loan over an extended period of time with interest. The interest that you plan to pay back will depend greatly on your credit and loan history.

It is a good idea to keep a regular job while you start your business, as companies are more willing to give money to someone who has years of work behind him with a particular company. Most banks will not loan money to individuals without at least two years with a particular company or business and at least five years of working in the same industry.

Many lenders, even after all the preliminary specifications are met, may ask for some type of collateral: your home, car, or other expensive item they will be able to sell to pay back your loan.

Equity Investments

Equity investments are just one other way to seek funds from investors if your startup loans have failed. Equity investors buy a piece of your business and become co-owners, which means they will also reap the rewards of your hard work. Many equity investors will ask for some type of collateral in case the business fails; doing so is not advisable. It is too risky for someone just starting out. If this is something that has developed, ask an attorney to take a look at the benefits the investor wants and have the attorney advise you on the steps you should take with this potential investor.

Bank Revolving Line of Credit

Home equity lines of credit are great ways to get the money needed to start your business, as they will not only give you the money you need, but will save you from getting more than you need.

Additional Forms of Financing

Just because you would rather not go through a bank or investment company, do not throw aside these other thoughts on financing without considering them thoroughly.

Personal Savings

Having personal savings can help you get on track. When starting a business there is no better time to take that out and use it. Sometimes you have to spend money to make money.

Friends/Colleagues

No one likes to ask friends, family, or colleagues for money, but if you can actually make them some money in the end they may be more willing. If you know of a friend, colleague, or family member that has some extra cash, ask them to help out your business. You will have to make it worth their while and offer something in return for their initial investment.

Other Business Owners

Other business owners could also be a good place to seek out small loan amounts. They were once in your shoes attempting to make their dreams come true. If you will be getting a loan from other business owners, you will have to legalize everything, and you will have to have a lawyer draw papers up indicating the loan amount, interest amount, and repayment details.

Grants for Small Businesses

There are grants available for your small business, but be aware of the scams associated with them. Grant information is available for you free of charge at any local library. You will have to go to the library's grantsmanship center, which is normally located in the business and resources section. Ask a librarian for help.

ONLINE RESOURCES FOR GRANTS	
http://www.gpoaccess.gov/fr/index.html	
http://foundationcenter.org/pnd/21century	
http://12.46.245.173/cfda/cfda.html	
http://usgovinfo.about.com/library/weekly/blgrantsources.htm	
A guide to help you understand how to raise capital and comply with the federal securities laws:	www.sba.com For Teens specifically: www.sba.gov/teens
Youth Venture	http://www.youthventure.org.
Online network for small businesses	http://www.gobignetwork.com/
Inc. offers daily resources for entrepreneurs	http://www.inc.com
Entrepreneur Mag offers a ton of resources and links for those staring or expanding a business	www.entrepreneurmag.com
Association of Collegiate Entrepreneurs	http://oak.cats.ohiou.edu/~ace/index.html.
Nonprofit organization dedicated to supporting students preparing for careers in business and business-related fields	http://www.fbla-pbl.org
Offers resources to the business needs of Generation X entrepreneurs with information, advice, and fun	http://www.businessownerside-acafe.com/genx
Profiles of business owners who started their businesses while students, along with numerous resources for young entrepreneurs	http://www.inc.com/search/20808.html.
Provided to educate and inspire young people to value free enterprise, business, & economics to improve the quality of their lives	http://www.ja.org
Offers middle and high school students with advice, quizzes, pro and con discussions of business ownership, and other business education resources	http://www.usmint.gov/kids/.

ONLINE RESOURCES FOR GRANTS	
Offers micro-enterprise development assistance, conferences, youth entrepreneur awards, technical assistance, more	**http://www.agnr.umd.edu/users/ kidbiz/nceyehist.html**
Students in Free Enterprise (SIFE	**http://www.sife.org**
YoungBiz	**http://www.youngbiz.com.**
Young Entrepreneur	**www.youngentrepreneur.com**
Young Entrepreneurs Network	**www.youngandsuccessful.com**
Young Entrepreneurs' Organization (YEO)	**www.yeo.org.**

Financing – Where to Apply for and Get Your Financing:

America's Business Funding Directory (http://www.business finance.com): This site provides a searchable database of potential lenders or investors for businesses, along with other information and resources related to funding.

SBA—Financing Your Business (http://www.sbaonline.sba. gov/financing/): The U.S. Small Business Administration works with banks and other institutions to provide loans and venture capital financing to businesses unable to secure financing through normal lending channels; this page describes the various programs available.

When Your Bank Says "NO!" (http://www.businessforum.com/ woods01.html): This site offers detailed advice and tips on how to prepare for seeking a business loan.

Venture Capital Resource Library (http://www.vfinance.com/): This site offers directories of venture capital firms, investment banks, angel investors, lenders, and sample business plans.

SUCCESS STORY: ART GUY DESIGN, INC.

Dana W. Ball of Arizona worked the majority of his career in the print design industry. "I grew weary of working for someone else, making money for someone else on their terms. I could never do that again. Also, my wife and friends got tired of hearing me complain and challenged me to put up or shut up. I put up," he says.

In 2003 Dana did just that and began his business, Art Guy Design, LLC. He offers creative solutions for living spaces with respect to remodeling, renovating, or new construction. "I run my business full-time. It wouldn't be fair to me or my clients to do it any other way," he says. Read more about him here or by logging onto **www.artguydesign.com**.

His business	I offer clients creative solutions to the spaces in which they live, whether they are considering a remodel, complete renovation, or new construction. Every homeowner deserves to live in a home that is thoughtfully designed. Bigger is not always better. A smaller home can and should use space efficiently, complement the owner's lifestyle, and express unique and artistic aesthetics.
How his idea was sparked	I have always been involved in the creative field – design, illustration – and have always possessed an interest in the design of the spaces in which we all work and live, and an ability to construct them. The metamorphosis to architectural design seemed natural and inevitable.
Why he started his own business	I prefer to define for myself the parameters under which I pursue my career and passion. I want to be accountable for and to myself. I want to be on the front lines of communication with clients and other professionals.
The pros and cons	It is challenging and I meet some very interesting people. It can be unpredictable.
His main concern in the first few years of business	I knew I was talented and capable, but I needed to fill my client pipeline and rev up my referral engine. Fortunately, I enjoy the unique challenges of being my own boss – participating in intelligent conversation with someone I've just met, taking risks that lead to personal growth, and always maintaining a positive attitude.
Business Type	Limited Liability Company

SUCCESS STORY: ART GUY DESIGN, INC.

His business base	It is a virtual business. I work from my home office and collaborate as necessary with other professionals. Every job is different and requires the skills and abilities of various experts. When needed, the local Starbucks serves well as my office.
Saw a steady income flow...	After the first two years, I started to feel the seeds of success beginning to grow and bloom .
His likes and dislikes about running a business	I look forward to the new challenges and adventures that each day brings. Every day is different. I am not naturally a "business" person, though I do find the learning curve interesting and unpredictable.
Qualities that have helped in business	I believe that I possess the courage of my convictions, the ability to pursue my goals and take the necessary risks, and the passion to do it with integrity and skill.
Future aspirations for his business	I am certain that every home can and should convey thoughtful design and artful aesthetics, and every homeowner can and should live in the home that they love, not the home that the next owner may love. I am also certain that this philosophy should permeate our culture to be the norm, not the exception. I am certain that I can advance this cause.
The key to his success	Persistence and talent, talent and persistence. If one isn't working, the other will.
Advice to new owners	Do it. Don't be afraid to fail. Fail forward. You succeed just by trying.
His business day	I work, on average, 60-70 hours per week, yet strive for a good work/life balance. To that end, I take time when necessary to get away, relax, and unwind. Clients understand as long as there is good communication.
The ease of breaking into his industry	No. As a society, we have allowed ourselves to accept mediocrity. We convince ourselves that the cheapest option is the most sensible. And we don't understand or appreciate the value of quality. It is at times difficult to educate clients otherwise.

SUCCESS STORY: ART GUY DESIGN, INC.	
The potential earning in his industry	Follow your passion and the money will come.
He believes it takes to be successful in business	Talent, persistence, passion, ability to take risks, objectivity, open mind, healthy but not overbearing ego, a little naivety and a small amount of rebellion.
His support group	I have an excellent support group, particularly my wife. She is an experienced businessperson and a business coach. I couldn't do this without her. Also, I have friends who are self-employed with whom I can share experiences. Finally, I have a mentor. It is important to always spot opportunities for learning. We can never know everything.
When he knew business was a success	I knew I was good at it, and decided to do it.

Author Biography & Dedication

Heather L. Shepherd

Heather L. Shepherd is an author, screenwriter, freelance writer, teacher, and speaker. She has successfully started and operated a number of businesses from home while caring for her seven children. Her readers and audiences alike have found her rich and humorous content to be 100% accurate, entertaining and most important easy to use. She has written and spoke on a diverse array of subjects including finding the career that works best for your personality to healing from past demons. She resides in Austin, Texas with her family. You can visit her at **www.heathershepherd. com** or contact her directly at writing4peace@msn.com.

Dedication

This book is dedicated to all students who still have an entrepreneurial spirit. For those students who are focusing on their future now while still in school.

A special thank you goes to all the entrepreneurs, who took the time to share their stories of success and hardship with me, and tell me the advice they have given to emerging entrepreneurs. I wish to extend my heartfelt gratitude and my deepest appreciation for their time and encouragement.

In this dedication we, (the publishers and myself) wish to congratulate you on your decision to take a leap of faith. Those around you will soon understand that the hero is the man (or woman) who believes in himself or herself and takes that step toward financial and personal independence. It was for you this book was written.

Index